STING
EASY PIANO COLLECTION

Cover photo by Fabrizio Ferri

ISBN 978-1-61780-421-2

HAL•LEONARD®
CORPORATION

7777 W. BLUEMOUND RD. P.O. BOX 13819 MILWAUKEE, WI 53213

In Australia Contact:
Hal Leonard Australia Pty. Ltd.
4 Lentara Court
Cheltenham, Victoria, 3192 Australia
Email: ausadmin@halleonard.com.au

Visit Hal Leonard Online at
www.halleonard.com

ALL THIS TIME

Music and Lyrics by
STING

Saw the sad shire hors - es walk-

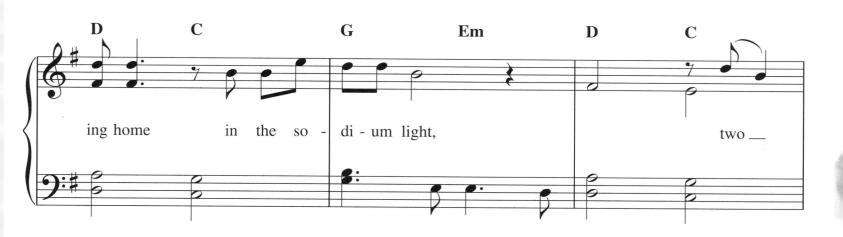

ing home in the so - di - um light, two ___

priests on the fer - ry. Oc - to - ber geese on a cold ___ win - ter's night.

All ___ this time ___ the

4

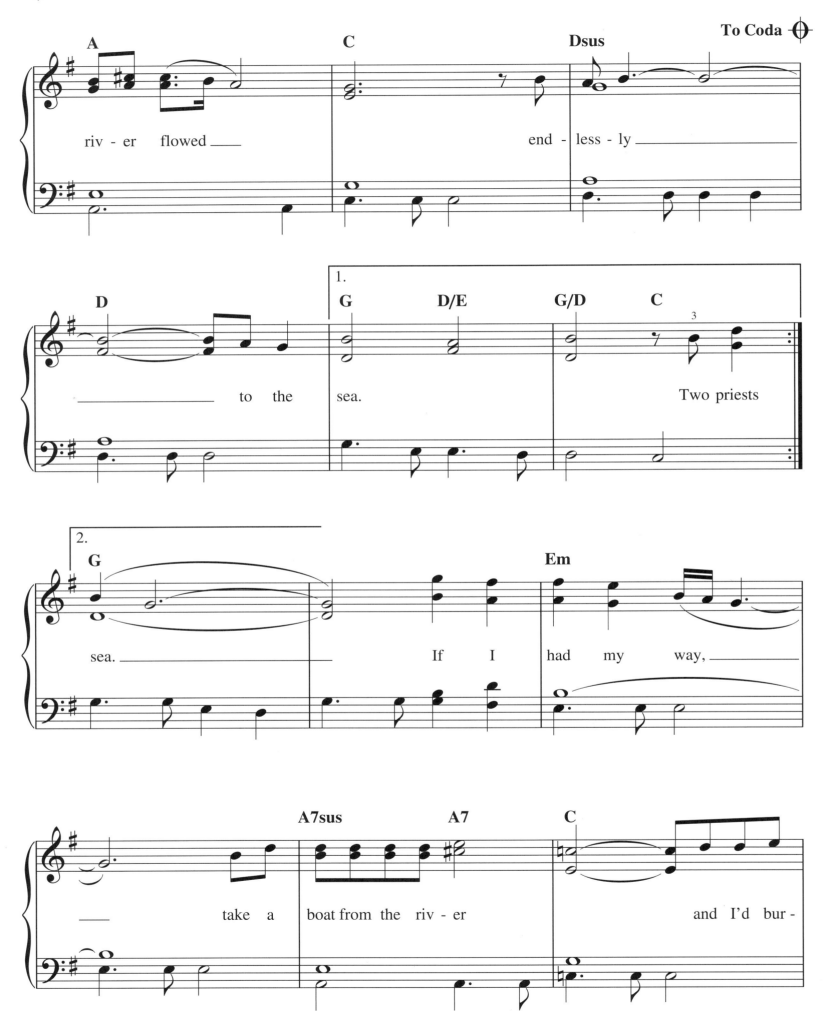

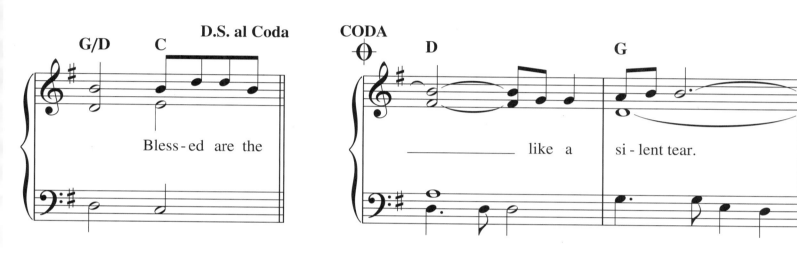

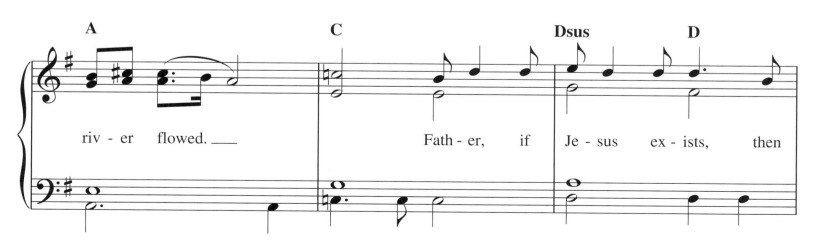

Additional Lyrics

Two priests came 'round our house tonight,
One young, one old, to offer prayers for the dying, to serve the final rite.
One to learn, one to teach which way the cold wind blows.
And fussing and flapping in the priestly black like a murder of crows.
All this time...

Blessed are the poor, for they shall inherit the earth.
Better to be poor than a fat man in the eye of the needle.
As these words were spoken, I swear I hear the old man laughing.
What good is a used-up world and how could it be worth having?
All this time...

Teachers told the Romans built this place.
They built a wall and a temple and an edge-of-the-empire garrison town.
They lived and they died. They prayed to their gods,
But the stone gods did not make a sound.
And their empire crumbled 'til all that was left were the stones the workmen found.

All this time the river flowed in the falling light of a Northern sun.
If I had my way, take a boat from the river.
Men go crazy in congregations, they only get better one by one.
One by one. One by one by one.

FIELDS OF GOLD

Music and Lyrics by
STING

Flowing, moderately
Bm7

Bm7

You'll re - mem-ber me ___ when the
stay with me, ___ will you

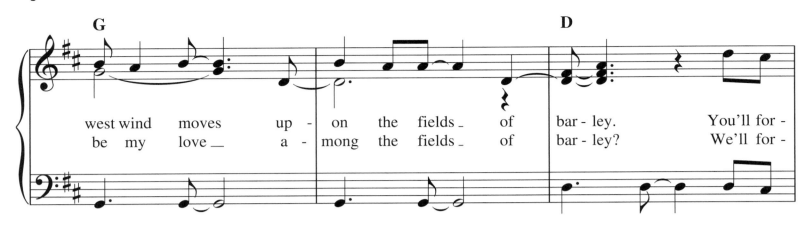

west wind moves up - on the fields __ of bar - ley. You'll for -
be my love __ a - mong the fields __ of bar - ley? We'll for -

get the sun __ in his jeal - ous sky __ as we walk in fields __ of
get the sun __ in his jeal - ous sky __ as we lie in fields __ of

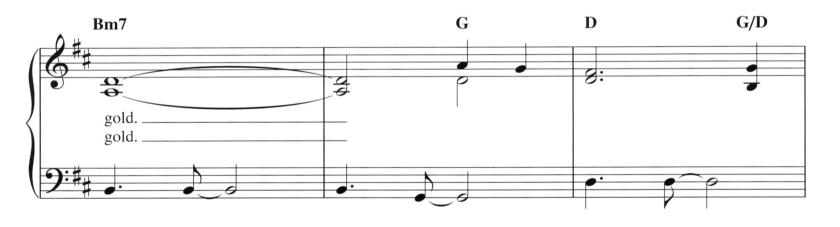

gold. _____
gold. _____

So she took her love __ for to gaze a - while __ up -
See the west wind move __ like a lov - er so __ up -

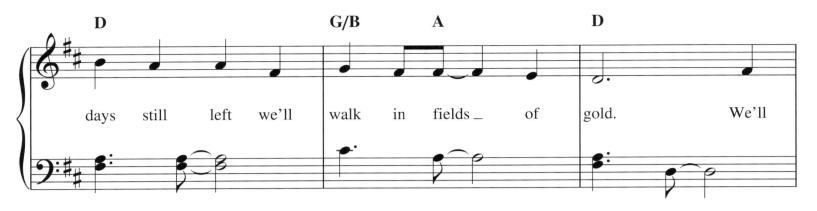

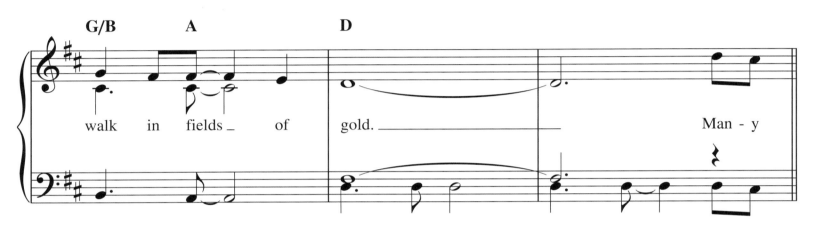

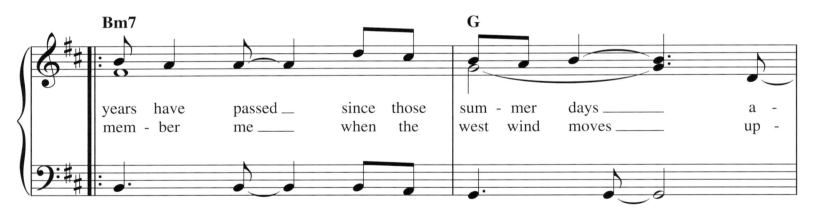

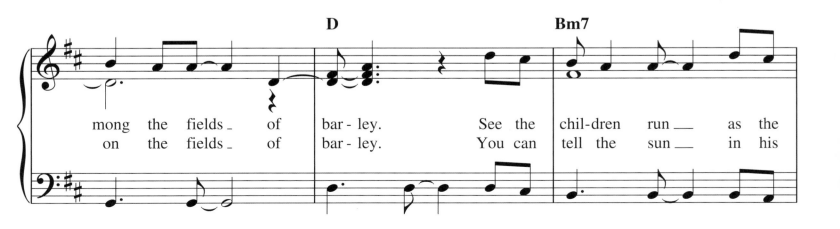

BRAND NEW DAY

Music and Lyrics by
STING

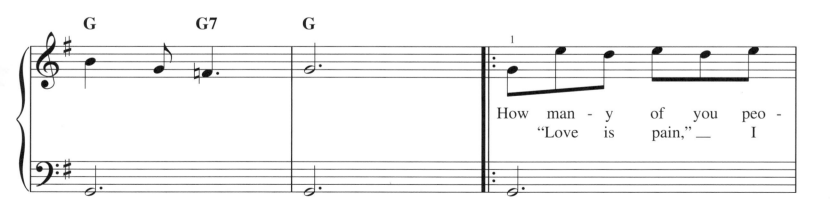

How man - y of you peo -
"Love is pain," __ I

ple out there been hurt in some kind of love af - fair? And
hear you say. "Love has a cruel _ and bit - ter way of pay - ing you

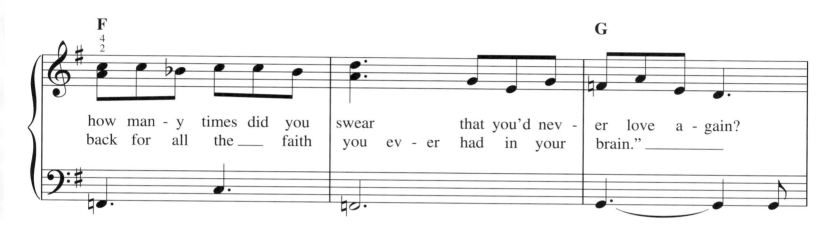

how man - y times did you swear that you'd nev - er love a - gain?
back for all the ___ faith you ev - er had in your brain." _____

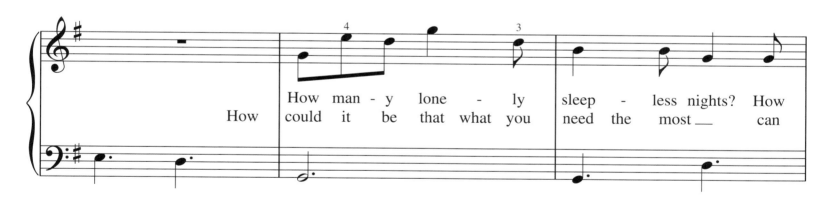

How
How man - y lone - ly sleep - less nights? How
could it be that what you need the most ___ can

man - y lies? ____ How man - y fights? ___ And why
leave you feel - ing just like a ghost? _____ You

would you wan-na put your-self___ through all of that a-gain?
nev - er wan-na feel___ so sad___ and lost___ a-gain?

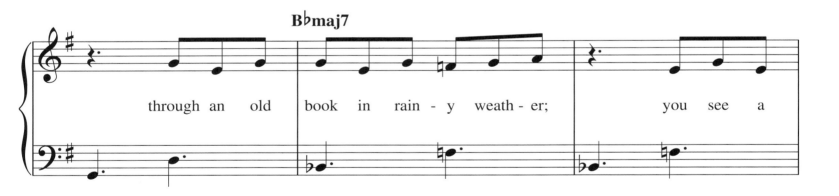

One day you could be look-ing

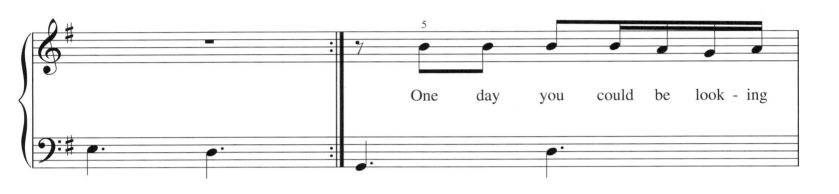

through an old book in rain-y weath-er; you see a

pic-ture of her smil-ing at you when you were still to-geth-er.

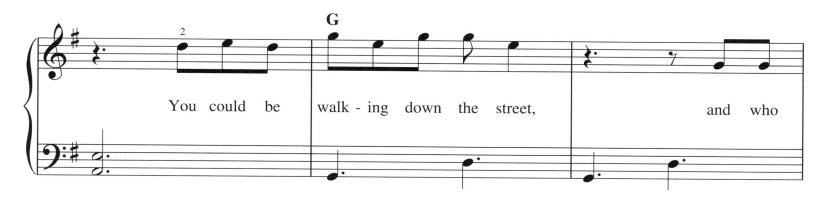

You could be walk - ing down the street, and who

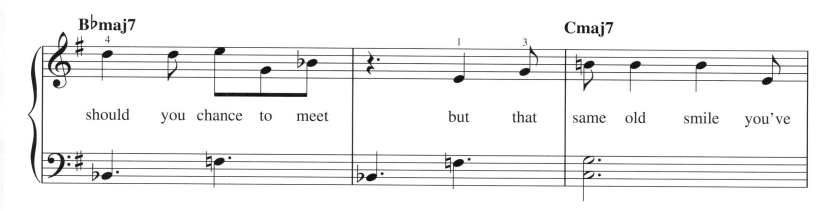

should you chance to meet but that same old smile you've

been think - ing of all day? Why don't we

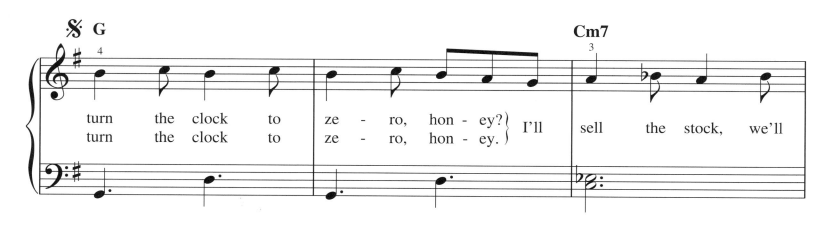

turn the clock to ze - ro, hon - ey?
turn the clock to ze - ro, hon - ey. I'll sell the stock, we'll

spend all the mon - ey. We're start - ing up a brand new

day. ___

Turn the clock all
Turn the clock to

the way back. I won - der if she'll take me back. I'm
ze - ro, Mac. I'm beg - ging her to take me back. I'm

think - ing in a brand new way.
think - ing in a brand new way.

Turn the clock to ze - ro, sis - ter. You'll
Turn the clock to ze - ro, boss. ___ The

nev - er know how much I missed her. I'm start - ing up a
riv - er's wide, ___ we'll swim a - cross. We're start - ing up a

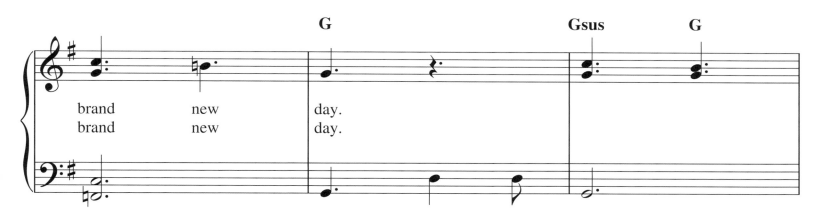

brand new day.
brand new day.

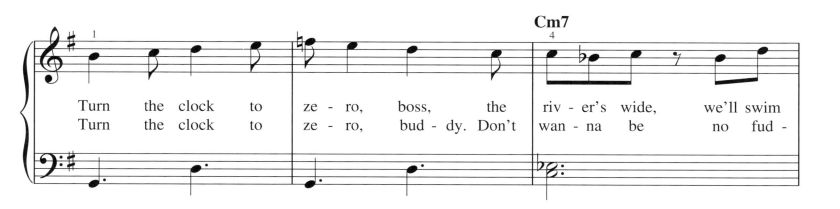

Turn the clock to ze - ro, boss, the riv - er's wide, we'll swim
Turn the clock to ze - ro, bud - dy. Don't wan - na be no fud -

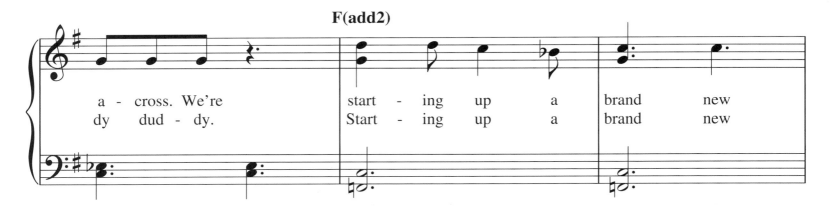

F(add2)

a - cross. We're / start - ing up a brand new
dy dud - dy. / Start - ing up a brand new

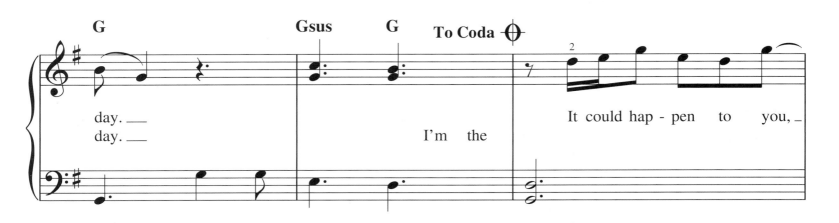

G **Gsus** **G** **To Coda** ⊕

day. ___
day. ___ I'm the It could hap - pen to you, _

E♭/G

___ just like it hap - pened to me. There's sim -

Csus **Am7**

ply no im - mun - i - ty, there's no guar - an - tee.

19

I say   love   is such a   force;   if you   find

your - self   in   it, babe,   need some time   for   re - flec - tion, you   say,

"Ba - by,   wait   a   min - ute,   wait   a   min - ute,

wait   a   min - ute, wait   a   min - ute,   wait   a   min - ute,

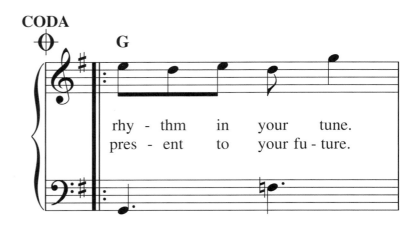

wait a min - ute." ___
And you can

rhy - thm in your tune.
pres - ent to your fu - ture.

I'm the sun and you're the moon.
You're the wound and I'm the su - ture.

I'm the
You're the

Fsus

bat and you're the cave.
mag - net to my pole.

You're the beach and I'm the wave.
I'm the dev - il in your soul.

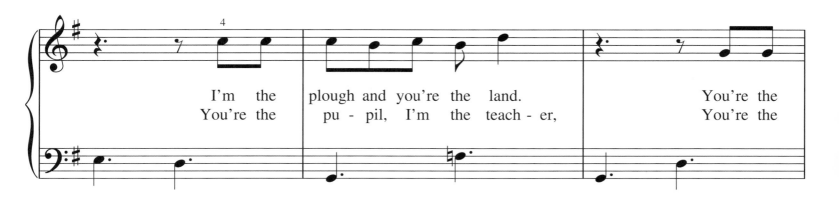

I'm the plough and you're the land.
You're the pu - pil, I'm the teach - er,

You're the
You're the

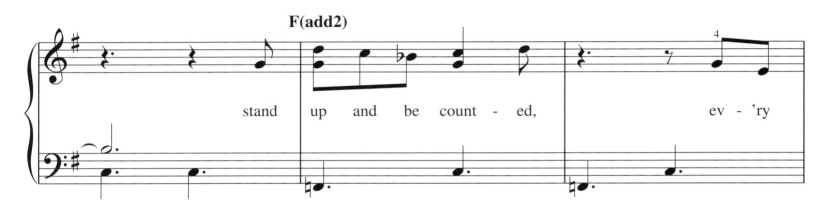

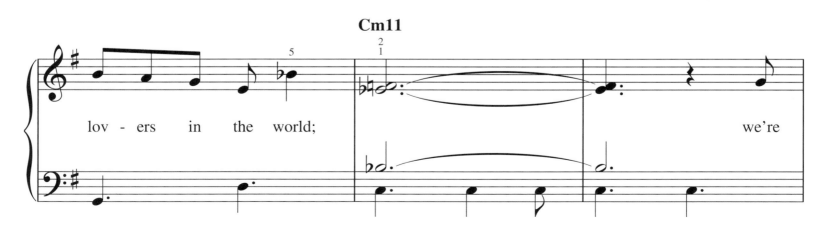

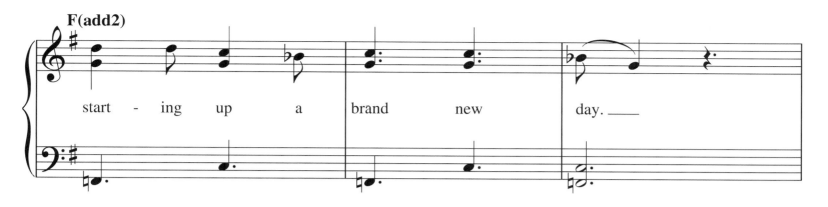

start - ing up a brand new day. ___

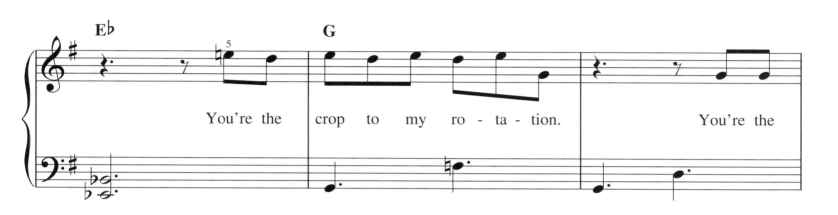

You're the crop to my ro - ta - tion. You're the

sum of my e - qua - tion. I'm the an - swer to your ques - tion.

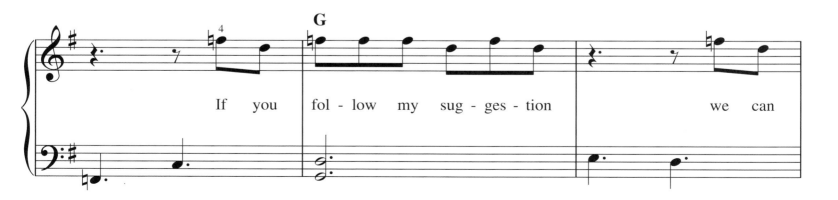

If you fol - low my sug - ges - tion we can

24

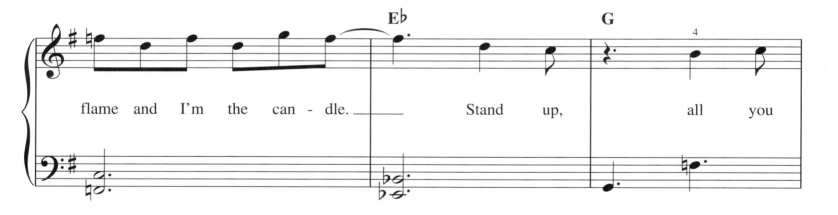

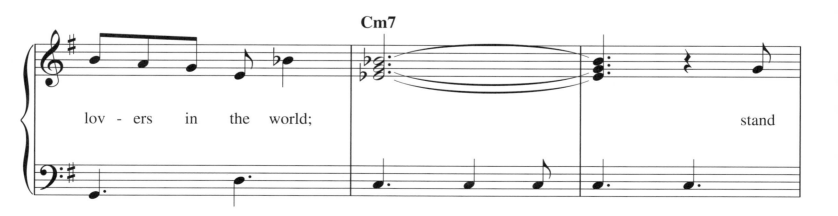

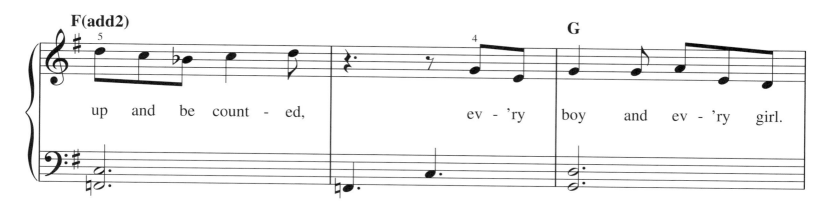

up and be count - ed,   ev - 'ry   boy   and   ev - 'ry   girl.

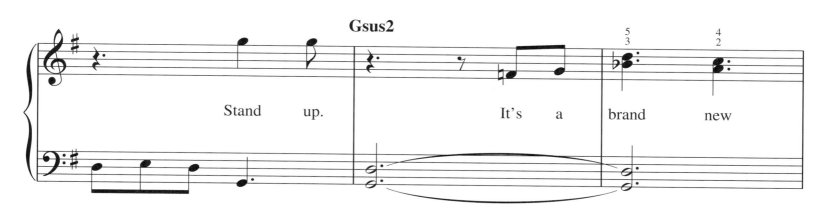

Stand   up.   It's   a   brand   new

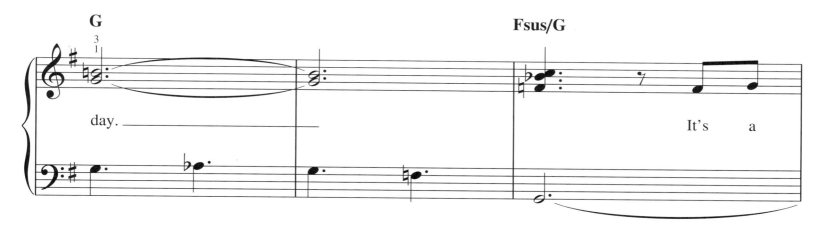

day. _____   It's   a

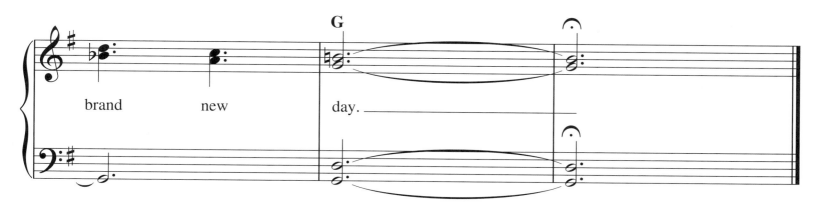

brand   new   day. _____

DESERT ROSE

Music and Lyrics by
STING

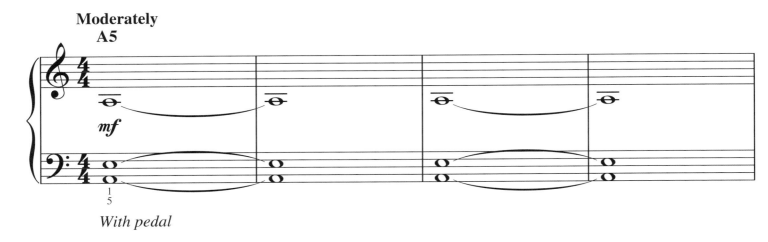

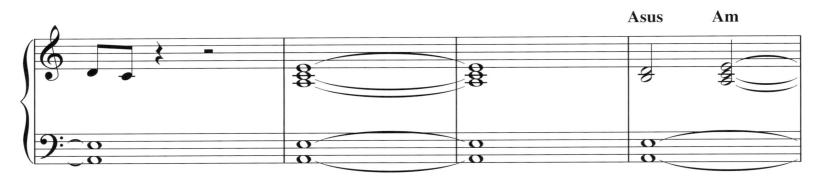

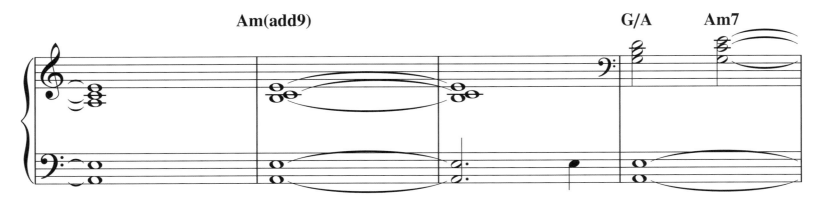

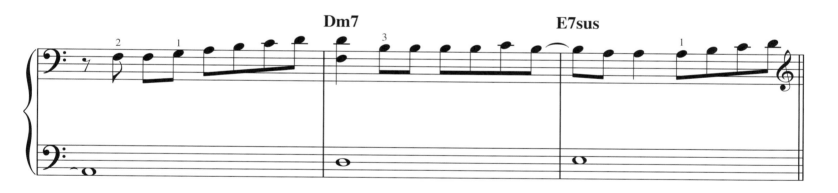

I dream of rain, e - lay, __ e - lay. __

I dream of gar - dens

28

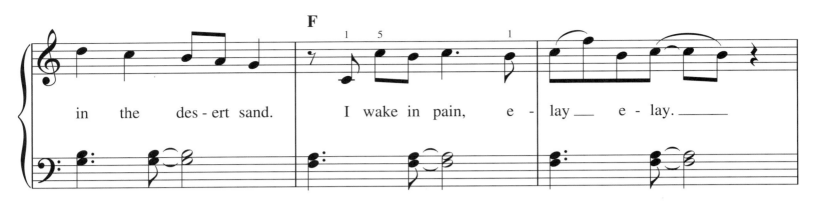

in the des-ert sand.   I wake in pain,   e - lay ___ e - lay. ___

Dm7   **E7sus**   **N.C.**

I dream of love   as   time runs through my hand.   I dream of fire,   e -

lay, ___ e - lay. ___   These dreams are tied   to   a   horse that will nev - er tire.

And in the flames,   e - lay, ___ e - lay. ___   Her shad-ows play   in   the

shape of a man's de - sire. This des - ert rose, e - lay, __ e - lay. __

Each of her veils, a se - cret prom - ise. This des - ert flower, e -

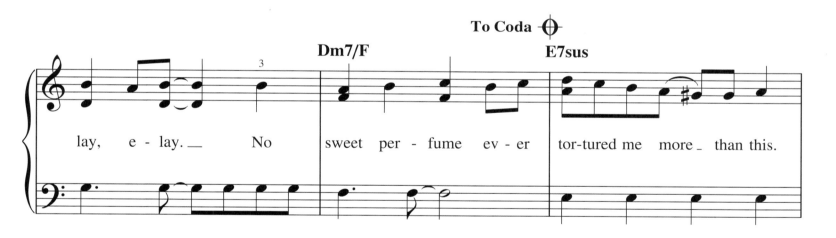

lay, e - lay. __ No sweet per - fume ev - er tor-tured me more _ than this.

And as she turns, e - lay, __ e - lay. __ This way she moves in the

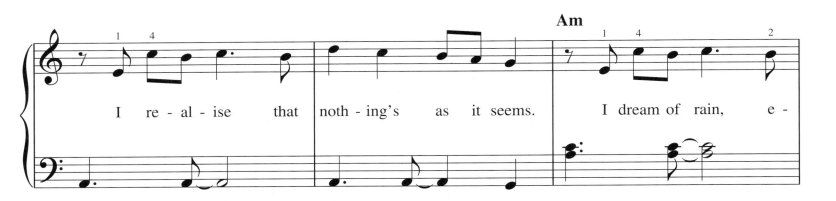

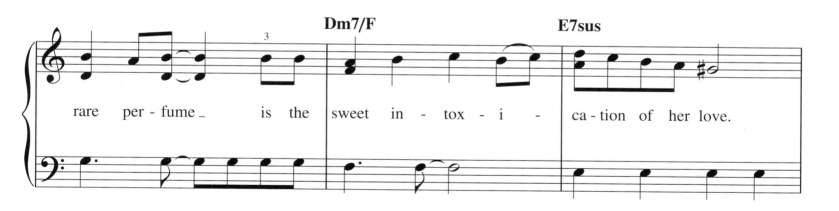

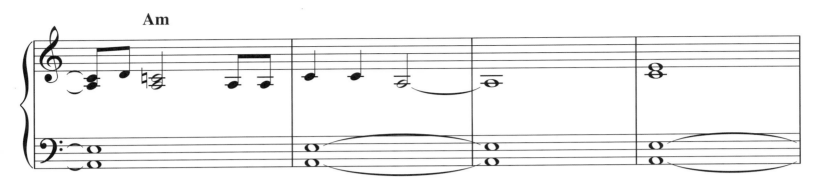

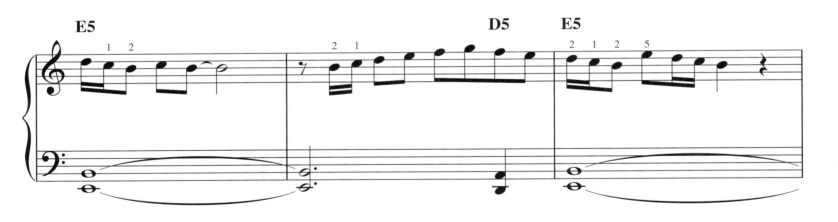

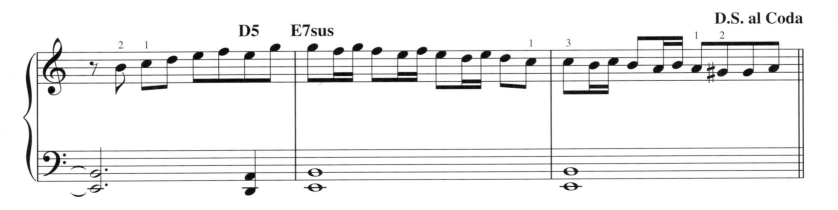

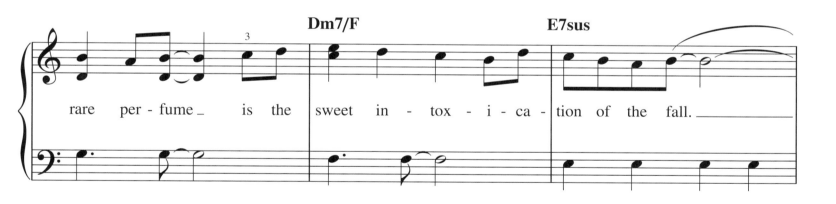

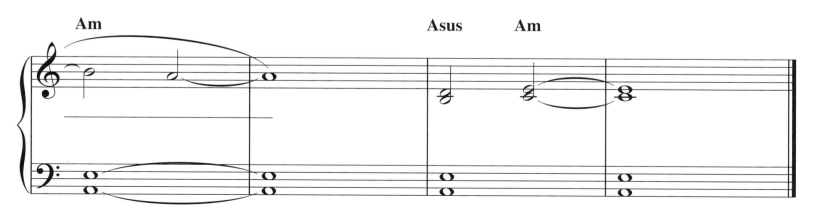

DON'T STAND SO CLOSE TO ME

Music and Lyrics by
STING

35

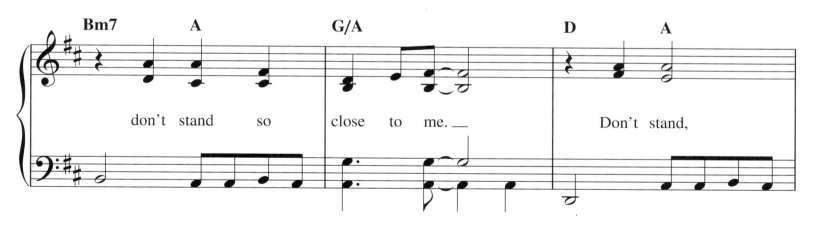

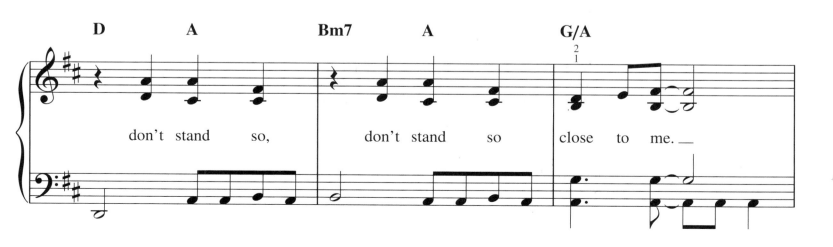

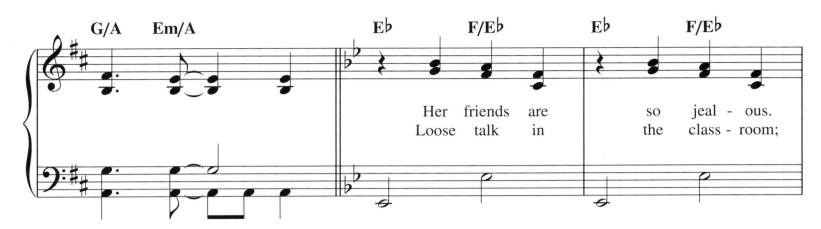

Her friends are so jeal - ous.
Loose talk in the class - room;

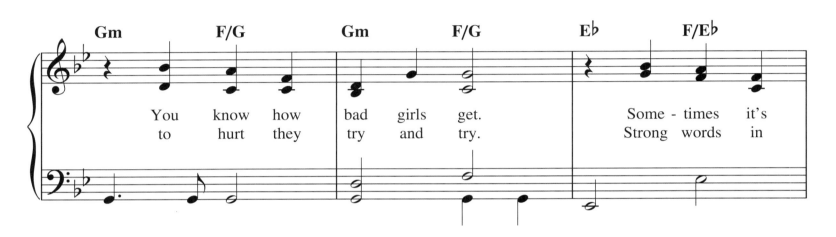

You know how bad girls get. Some - times it's
to hurt how they try and try. Strong words in

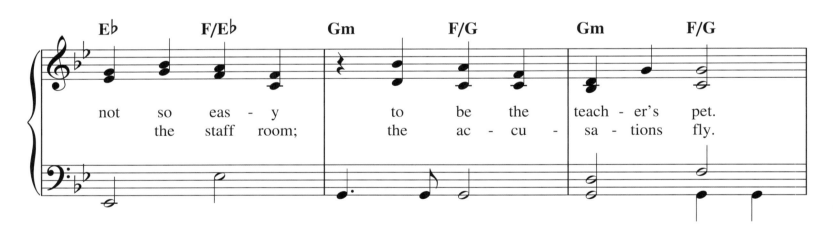

not so eas - y to be the teach - er's pet.
the staff room; the ac - cu - sa - tions fly.

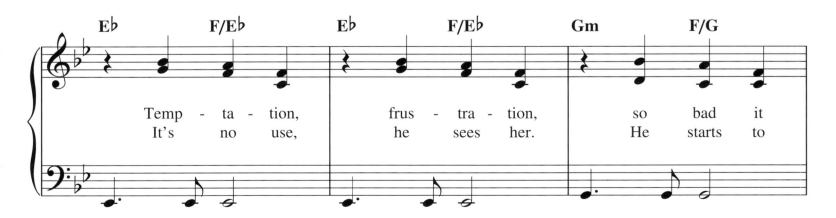

Temp - ta - tion, frus - tra - tion, so bad it
It's no use, he sees her. He starts to

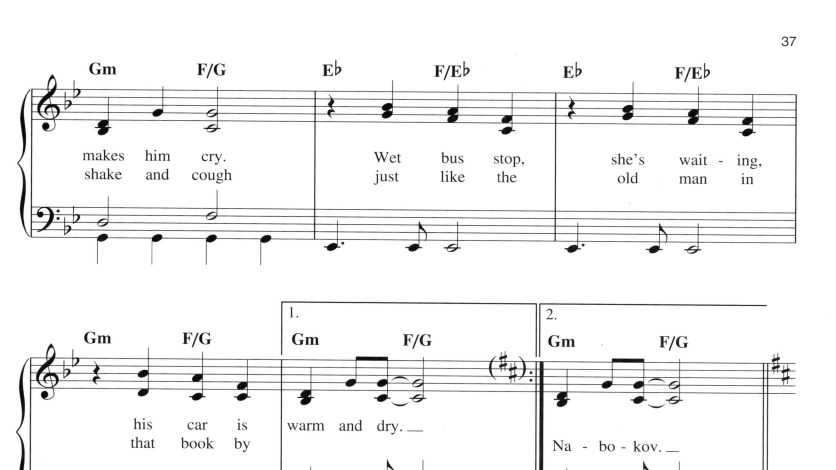

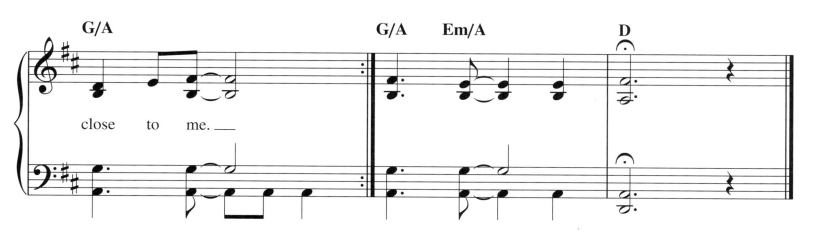

ENGLISHMAN IN NEW YORK

Music and Lyrics by
STING

39

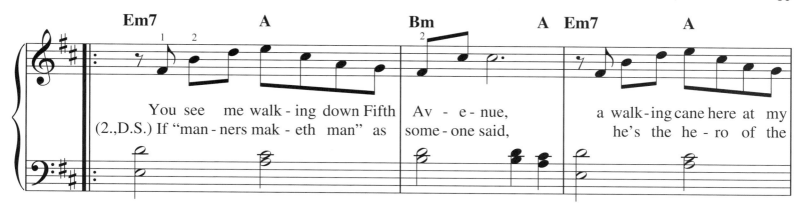

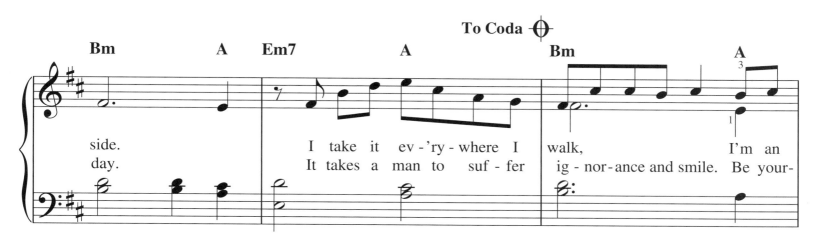

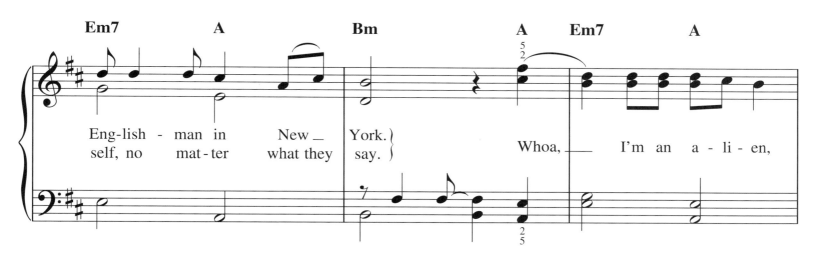

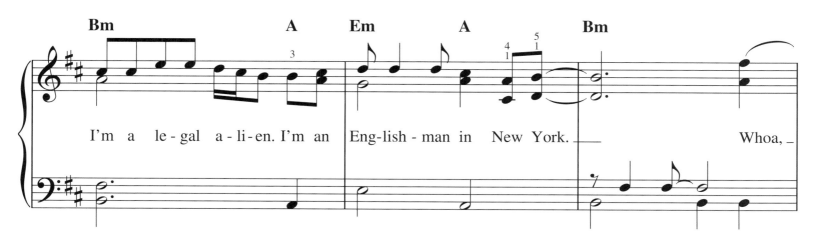

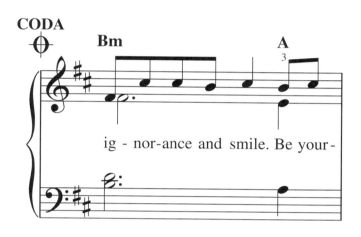

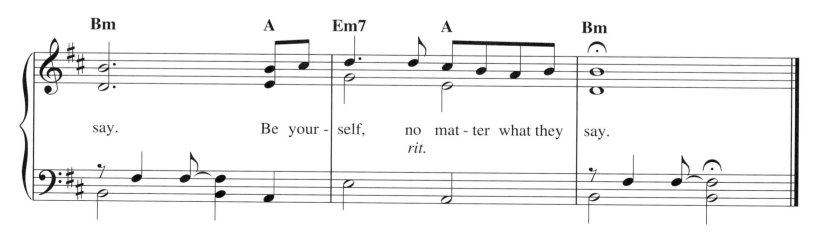

EVERY BREATH YOU TAKE

Music and Lyrics by
STING

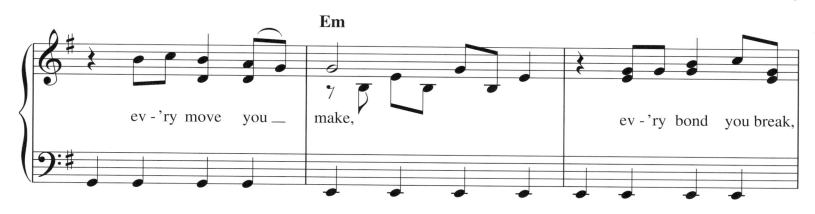

ev-'ry move you __ make, ev-'ry bond you break,

ev-'ry step you take, I'll be watch-ing you.

Ev-'ry sin-gle __ day, ev-'ry word you __

say, ev-'ry game you play, ev-'ry night you stay,

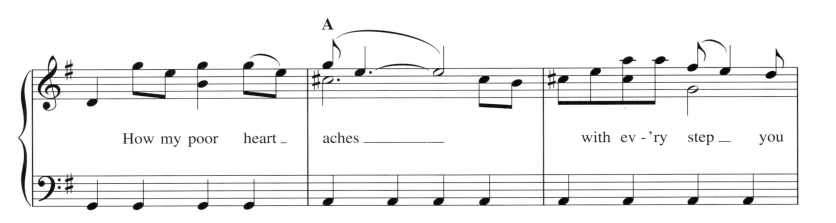

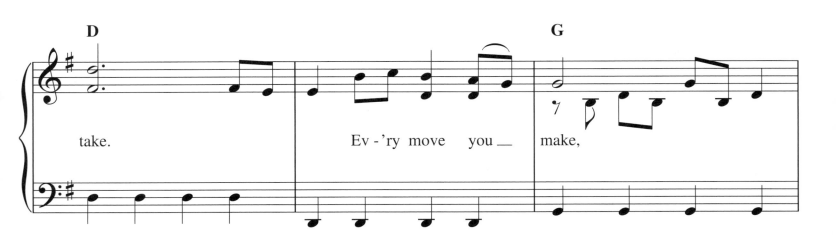

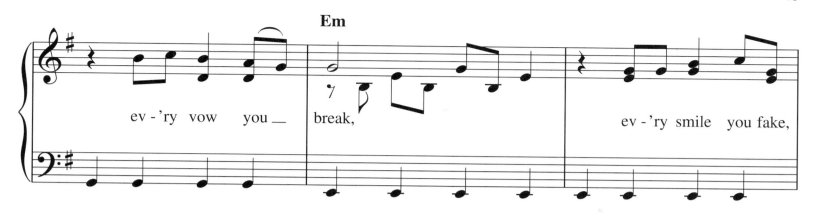

you I can't_ re-place. I feel so cold and I long for your_ em-brace.

I keep cry - ing ba - by, ba - by, please.

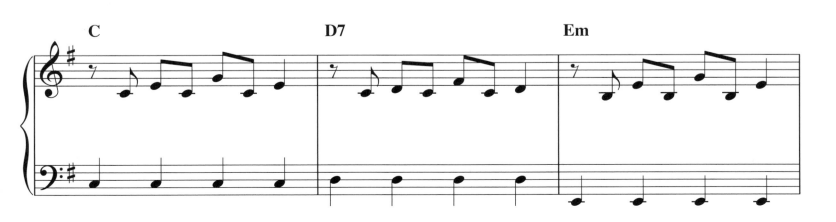

Oh, can't you ___

Ev - 'ry move you make,

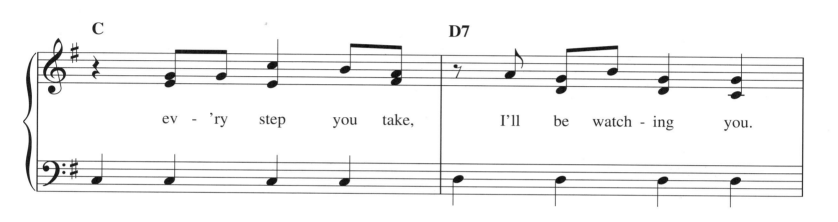

ev - 'ry step you take, I'll be watch - ing you.

I'll be watch - ing you.

IF I EVER LOSE MY FAITH IN YOU

Music and Lyrics by
STING

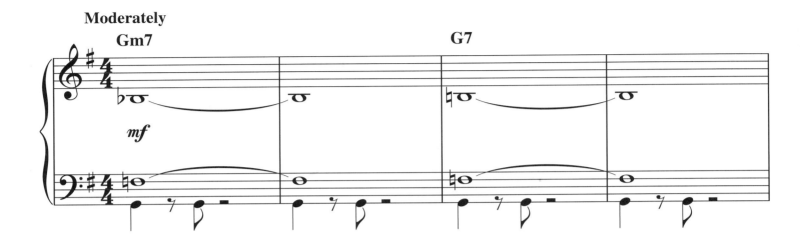

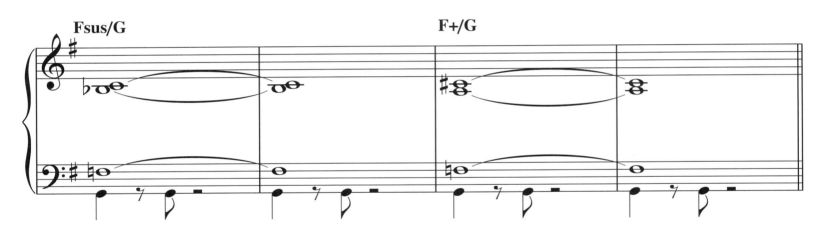

You could say I ____ lost my faith in sci - ence and prog-ress.
Some would say I was a ____ lost man in a lost world.
I nev - er saw no ____ mir-a-cle of sci-ence

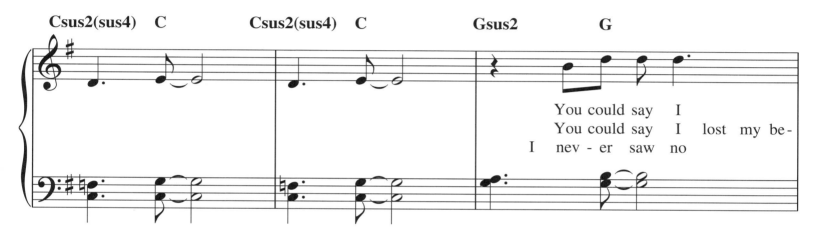

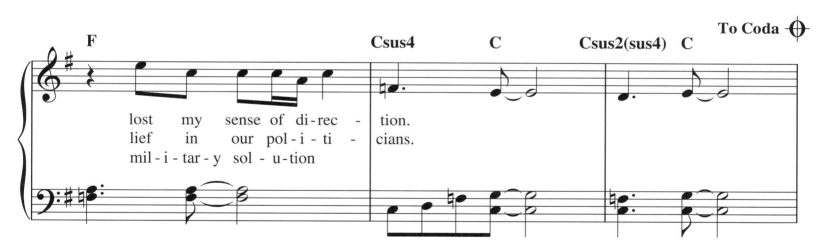

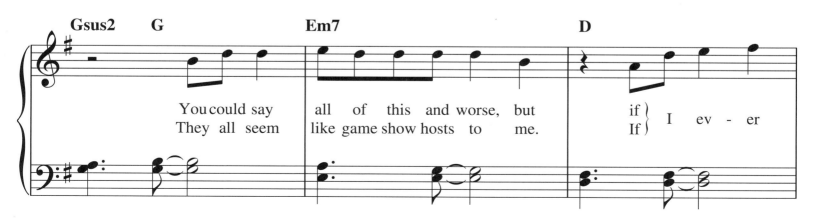

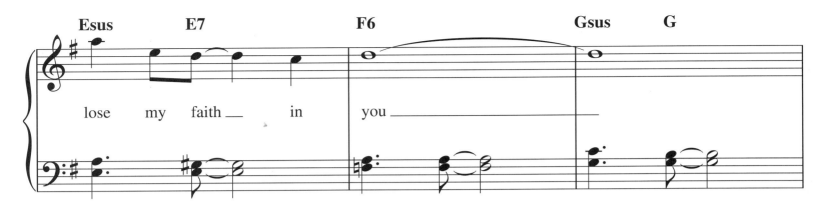

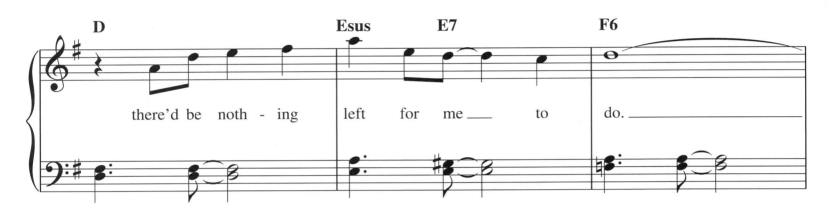

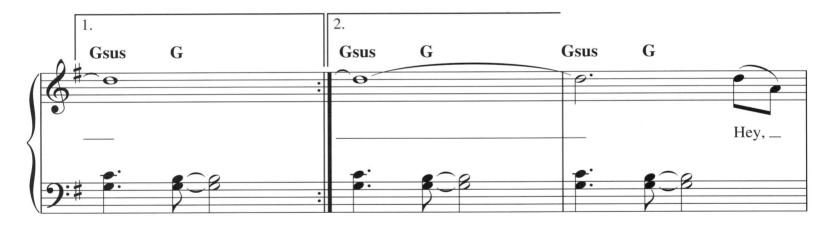

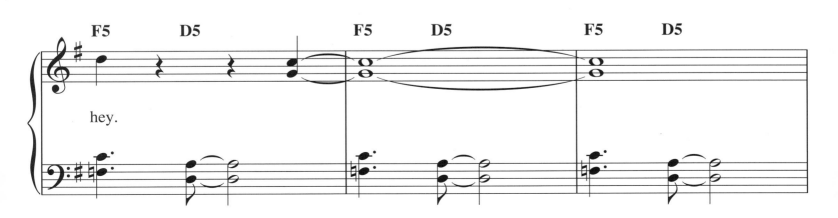

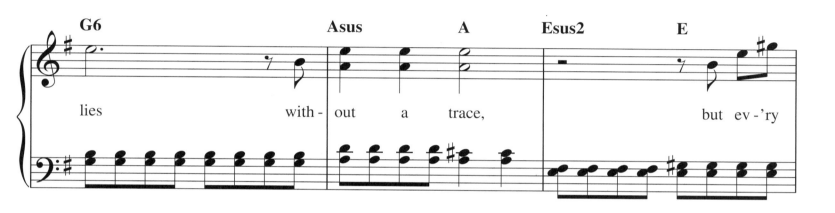

D.S. al Coda

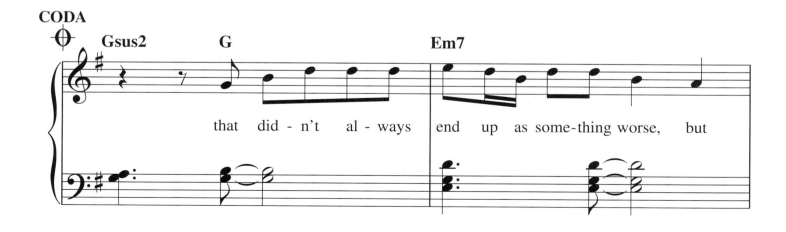

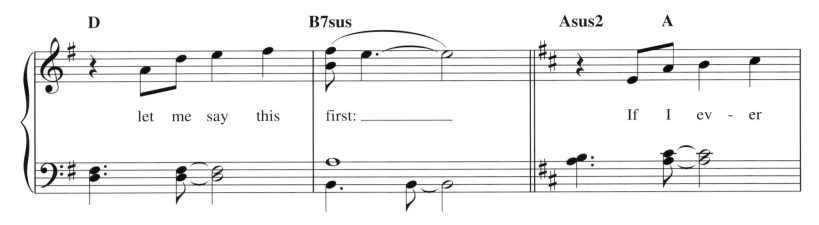

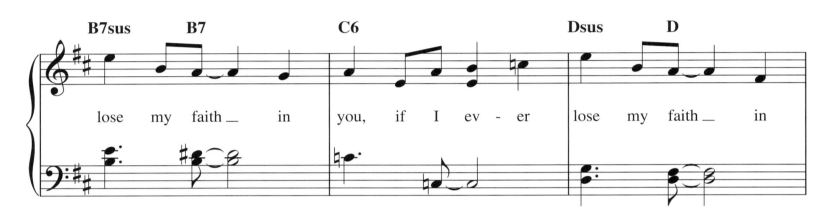

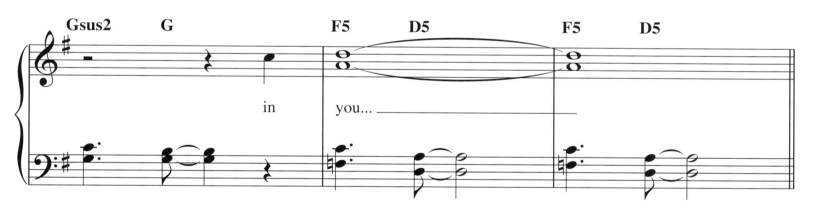

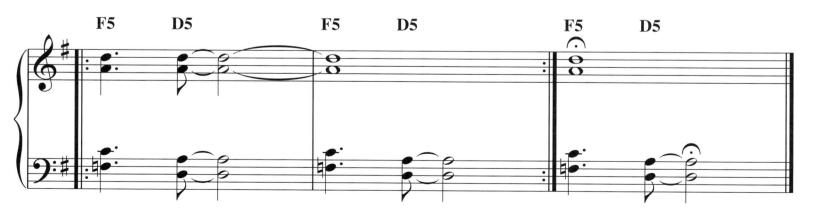

KING OF PAIN

Music and Lyrics by
STING

Moderately fast

There's a lit-tle black spot on the sun_ to-day;_ it's the same old thing_ as_ yes-ter-day._ There's a black hat caught_ in the high_ tree top;

there's a flag-pole rag ___ and the wind ___

___ won't stop. ___ I have

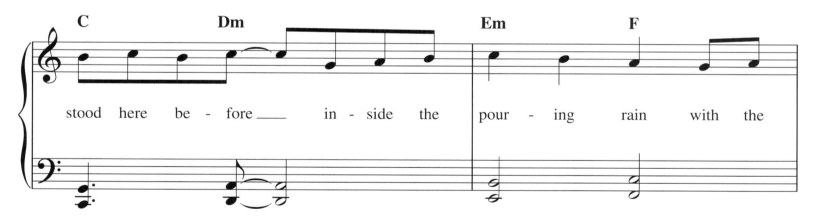

stood here be - fore ___ in - side the pour - ing rain with the

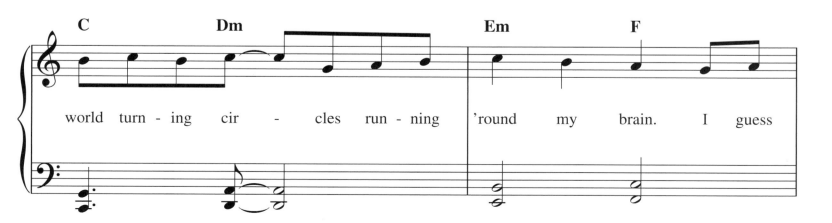

world turn - ing cir - cles run - ning 'round my brain. I guess

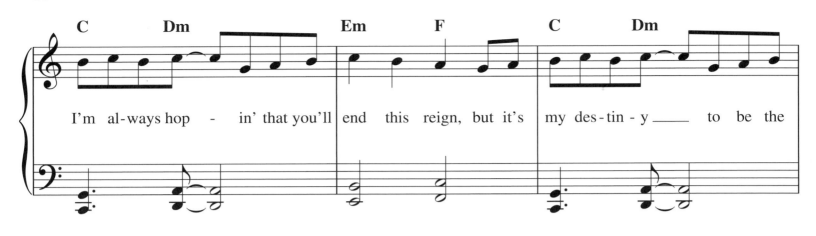

I'm al-ways hop - in' that you'll end this reign, but it's my des-tin-y _____ to be the

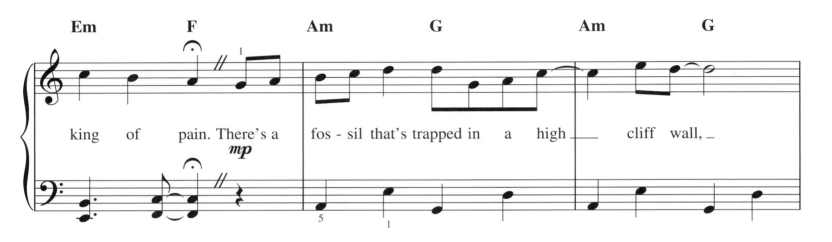

king of pain. There's a fos - sil that's trapped in a high _____ cliff wall, _

that's my soul _ up there. _ There's a dead sal - mon fro - zen in a

wa - ter - fall, _ that's my soul _ up there. _ There's a

57

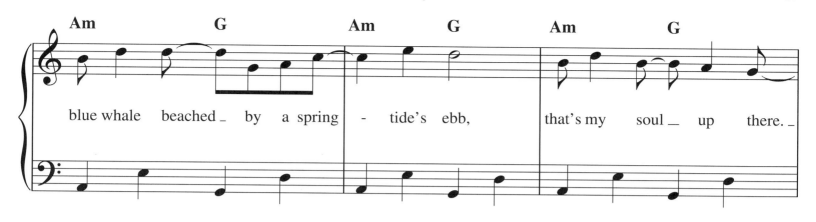

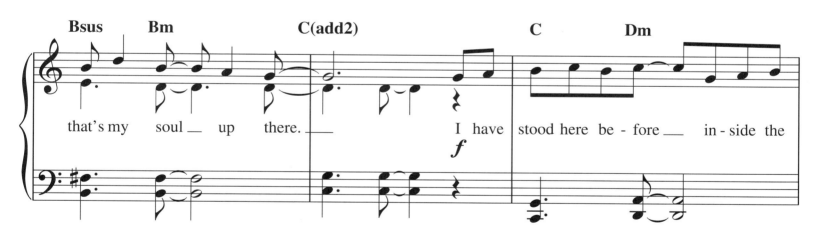

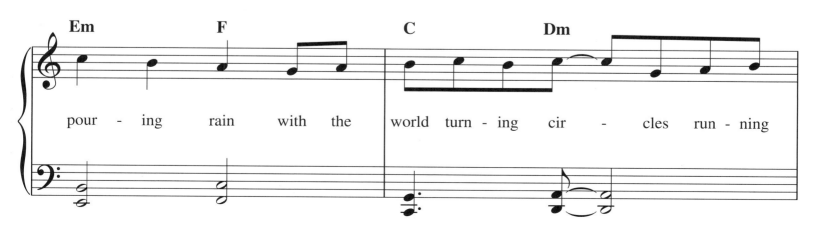

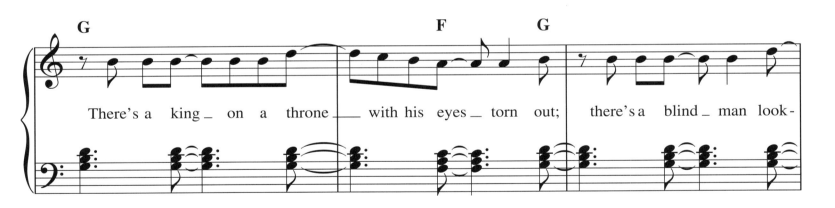

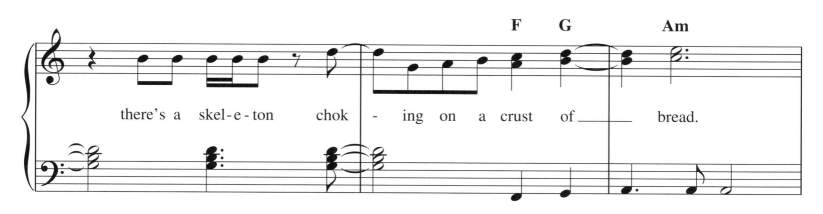

there's a skel-e-ton chok - ing on a crust of ____ bread.

There's a red fox torn __ by a hunts-

- man's pack, that's my soul __ up there. ___ There's a

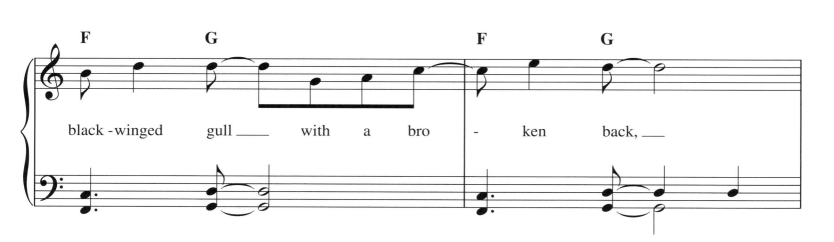

black -winged gull ____ with a bro - ken back, ___

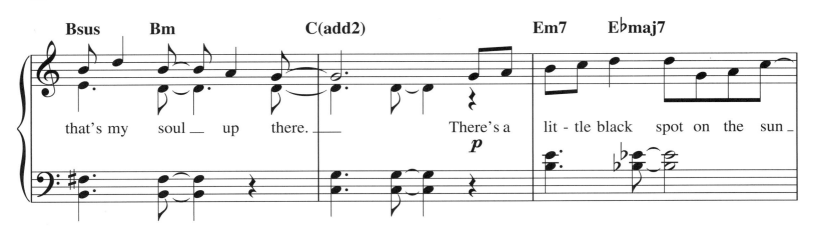

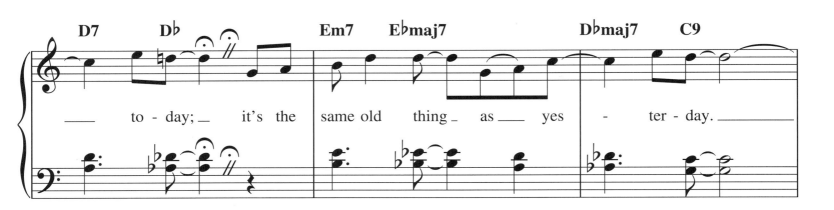

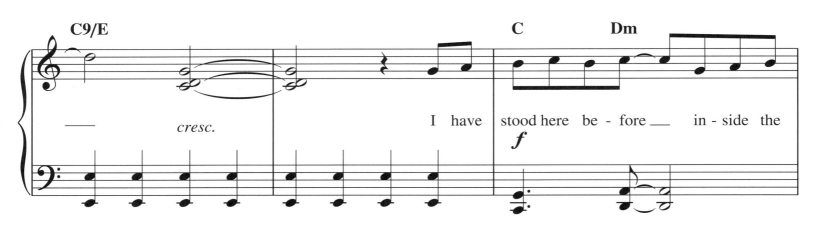

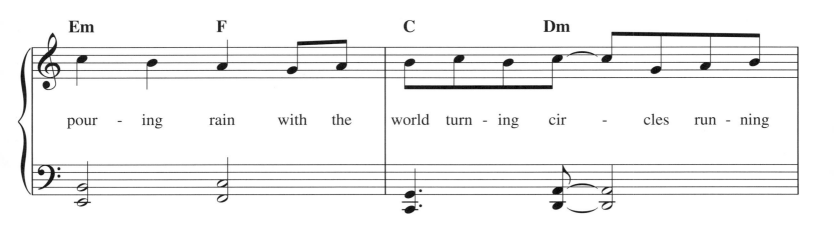

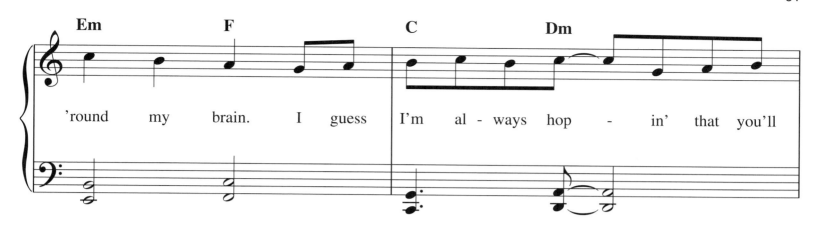

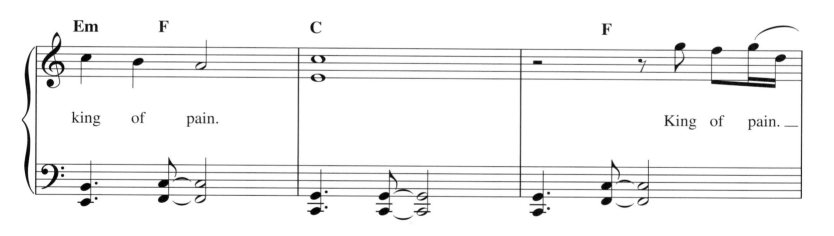

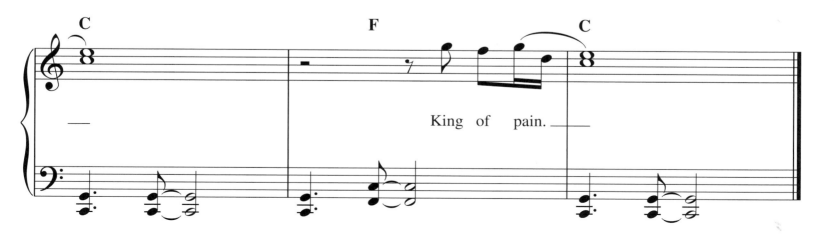

MESSAGE IN A BOTTLE

Music and Lyrics by
STING

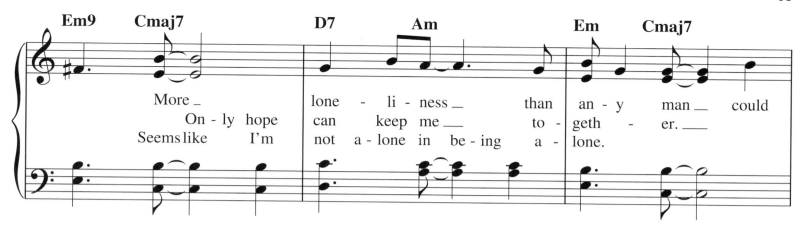

More _
On - ly hope can keep me _ to - geth - er. _
Seems like I'm not a - lone in be - ing a - lone.

lone - li - ness _ than an - y man _ could

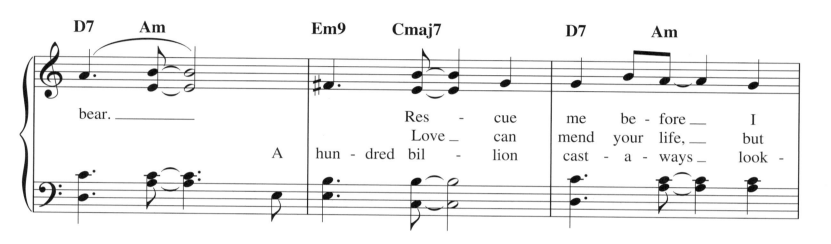

bear. _

Res - cue me be - fore _ I
A hun - dred bil - lion cast - a - ways _ look -

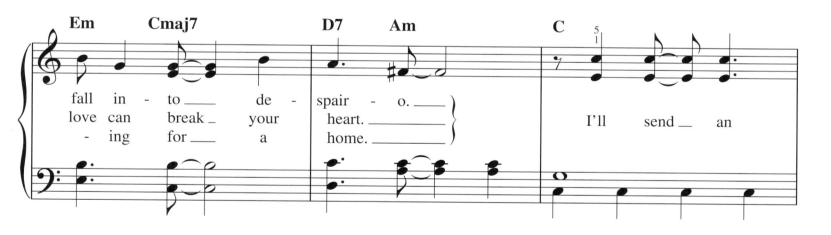

fall in - to _ de - spair - o. _
love can break _ your heart. _
- ing for _ a home. _

I'll send _ an

S. O. S. _ to the world. I'll send _ an

S. O. S. _ to the

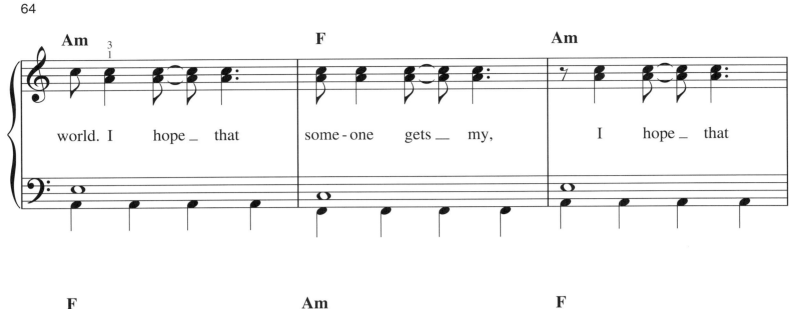

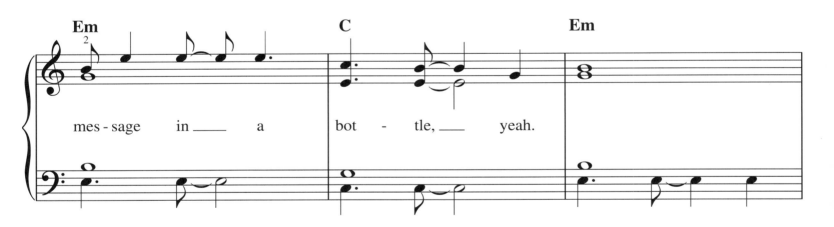

Mes - sage in ___ a bot - tle, ___ yeah.

SHAPE OF MY HEART

Music by STING and DOMINIC MILLER
Lyrics by STING

He deals the cards   as   a
He deals the cards   to
(See additional lyrics)

med - i - ta - tion ___   and those he plays nev-er sus - pect
find the an - swer, ___   the sa-cred ge - om - e-try of chance,

69

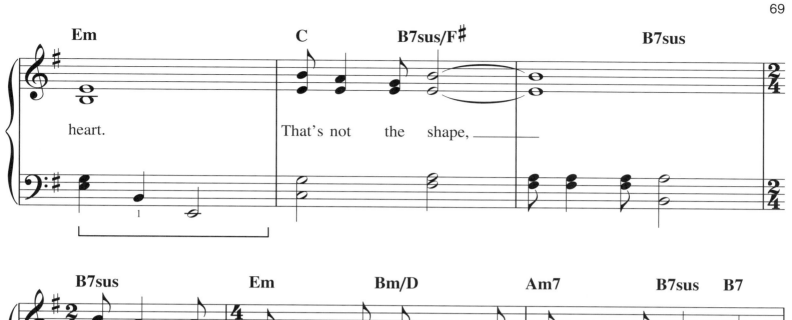

Additional Lyrics

And if I told her that I loved you,
You'd maybe think there's something wrong.
I'm not a man of too many faces.
The mask I wear is one.

Those who speak know nothing,
And find out to their cost
Like those who curse their luck in too many places,
And those who fear are lost.

I know that the spades are...

WRAPPED AROUND YOUR FINGER

Music and Lyrics by
STING

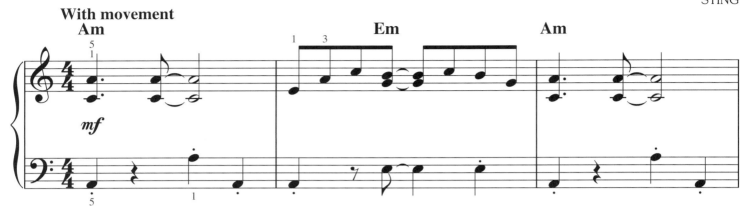

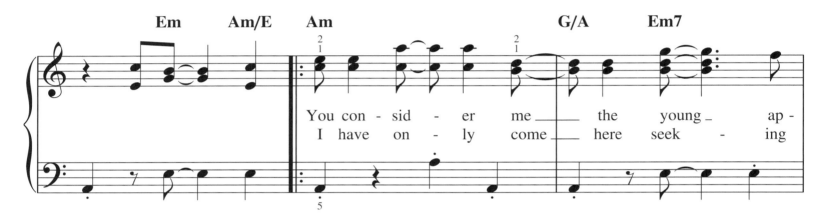

You con - sid - er me ____ the young ____ ap -
I have on - ly come ____ here seek ____ ing

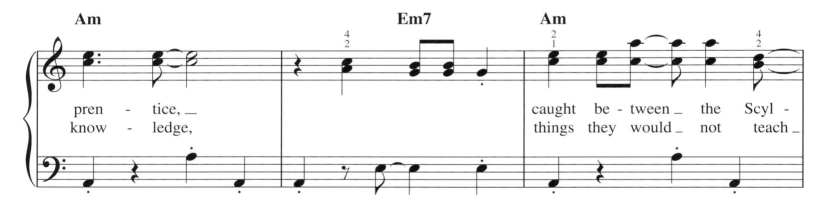

pren - tice, ____ caught be - tween ____ the Scyl -
know - ledge, ____ things they would ____ not teach ____

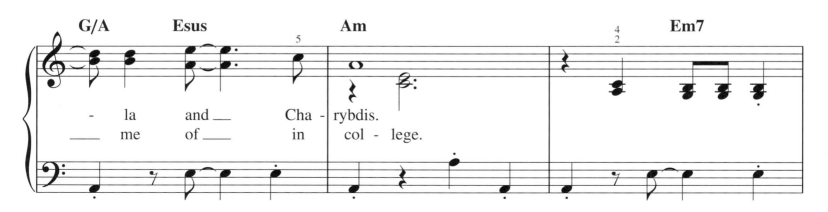

- la and ____ Cha - rybdis.
____ me of ____ in col - lege.

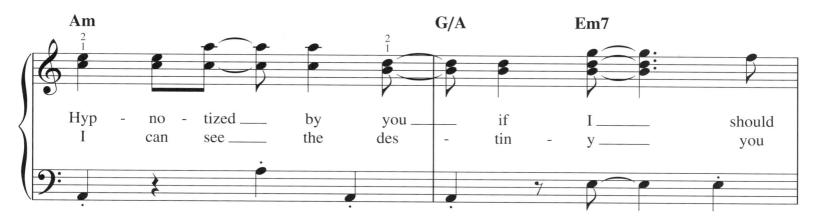

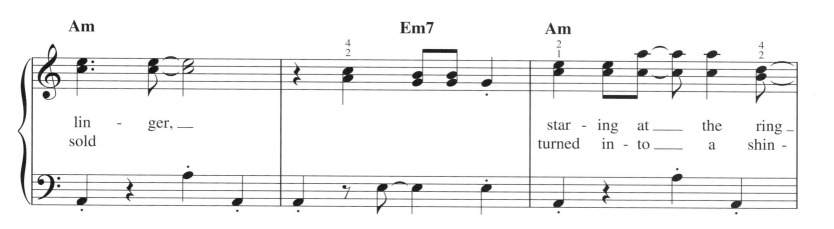

73

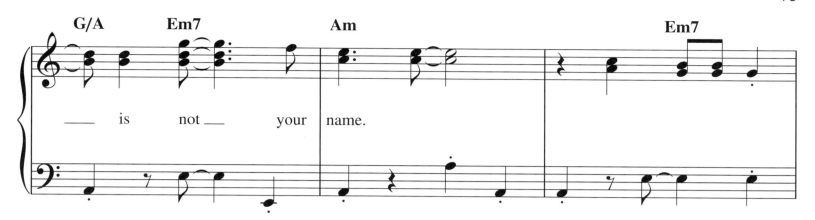

is not ___ your name.

I know what ___ you're up ___ to just ___ the same.

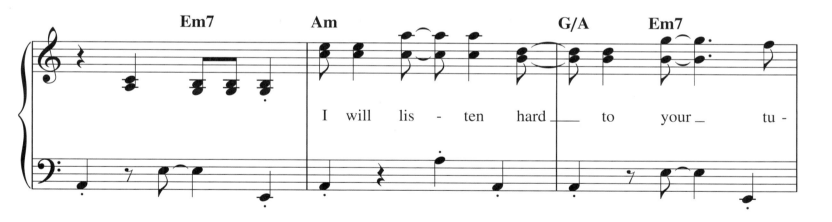

I will lis - ten hard ___ to your ___ tu -

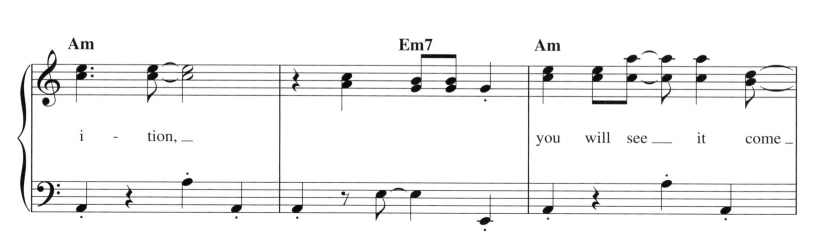

i - tion, ___

you will see ___ it come ___

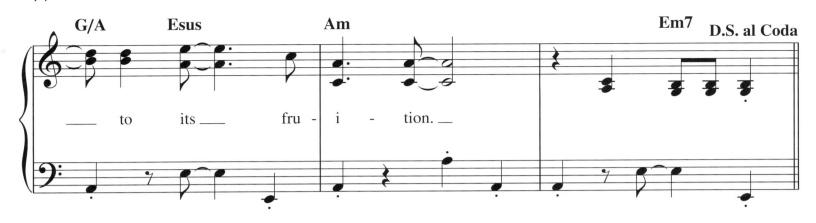

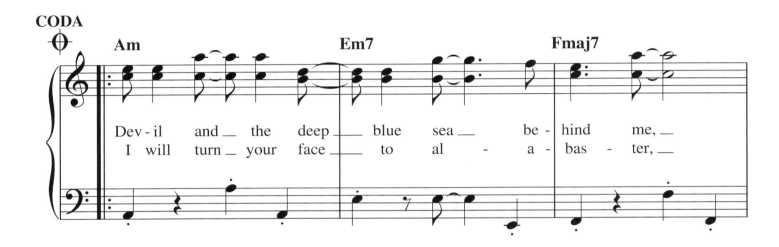

75

ROXANNE

Music and Lyrics by
STING

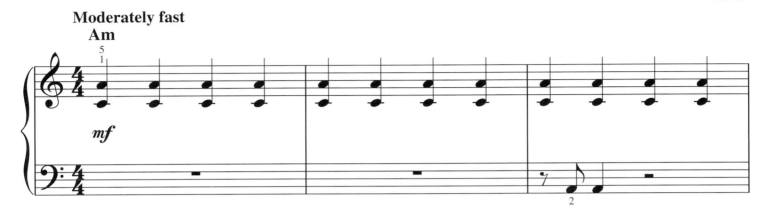

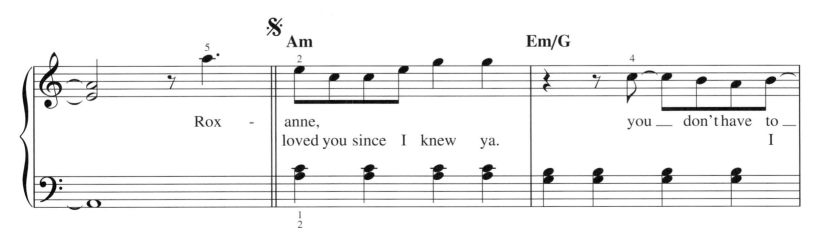

Rox - anne,
loved you since I knew ya.
you __ don't have to __
I

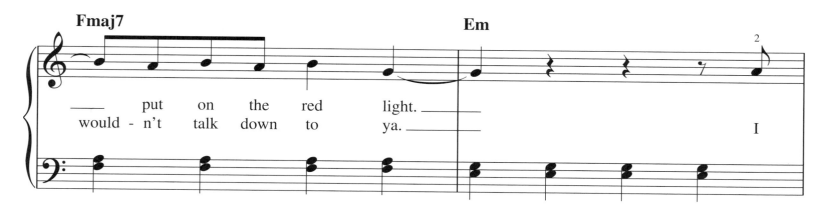

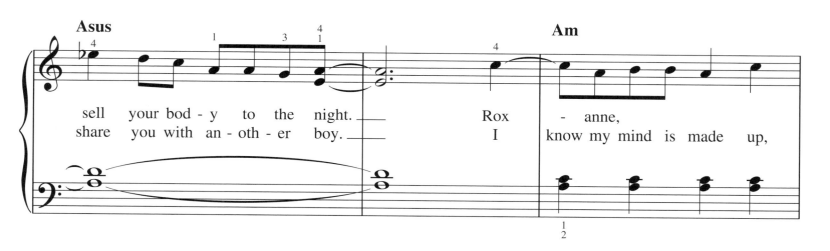

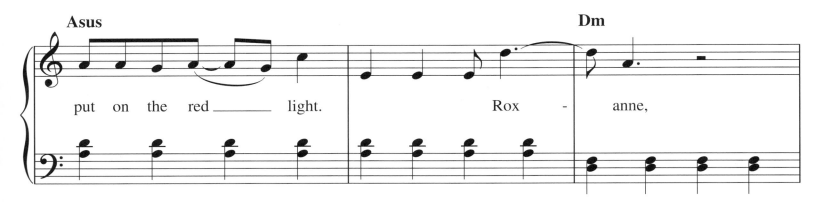

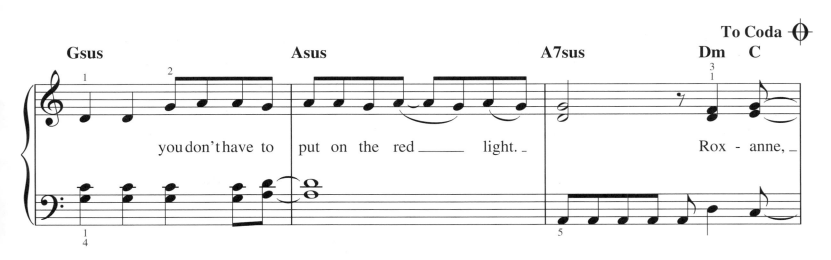

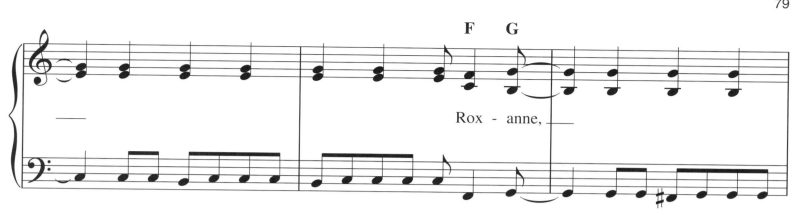

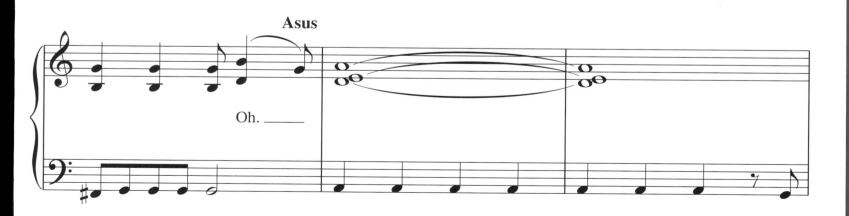

LITTLE FLY

Lyrics by WILLIAM BLAKE
Music by ESPERANZA SPALDING

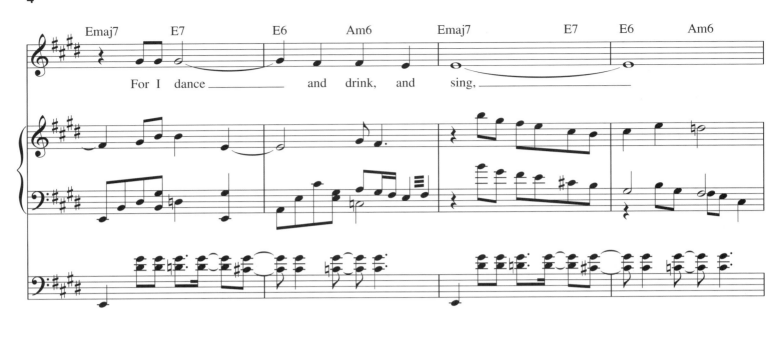

For I dance _____ and drink, and sing, _____

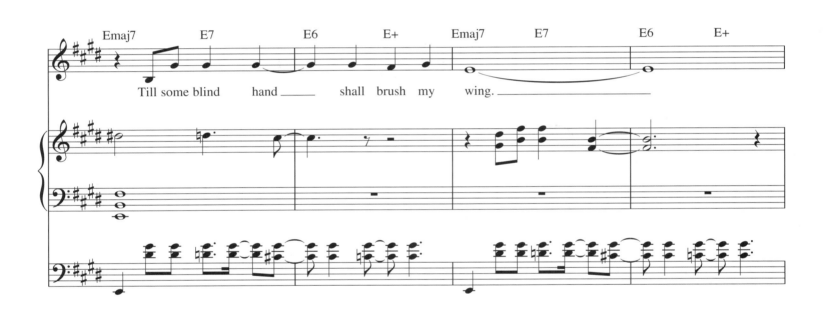

Till some blind hand _____ shall brush my wing. _____

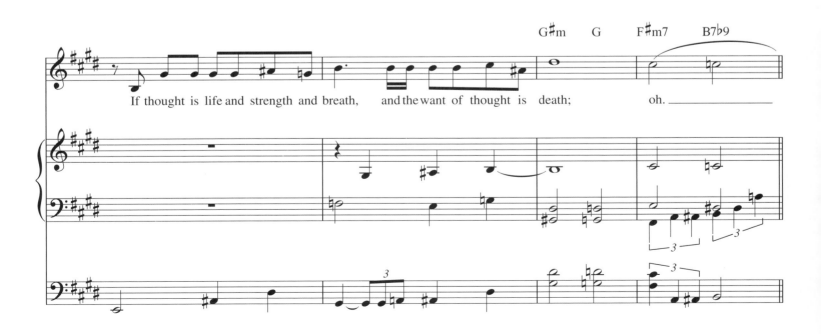

If thought is life and strength and breath, and the want of thought is death; oh. _____

Then am I a hap - py fly.

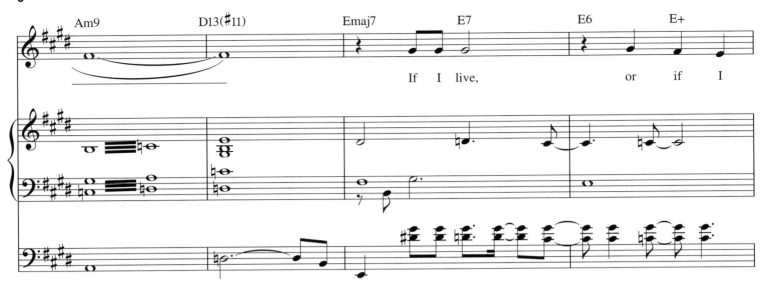

If I live, or if I

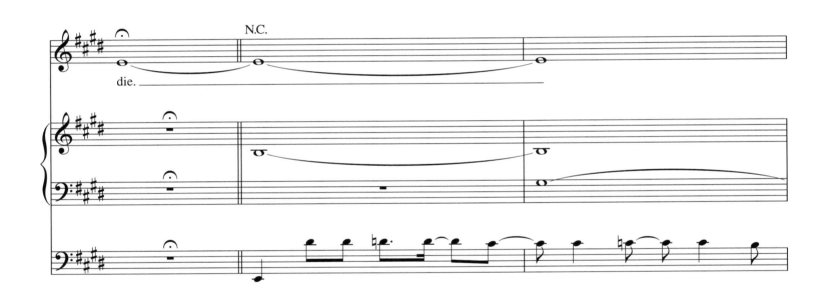

die.

KNOWLEDGE OF GOOD AND EVIL

By ESPERANZA SPALDING

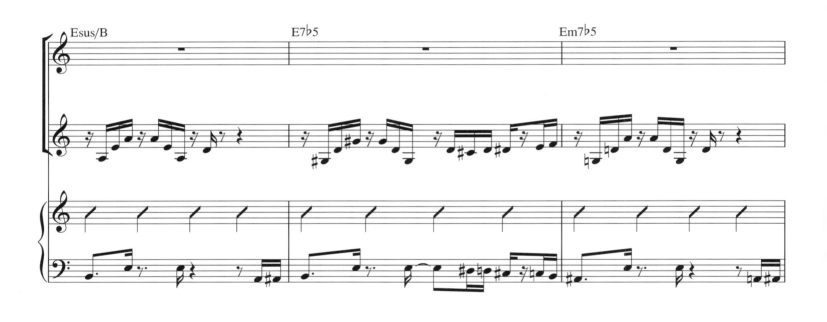

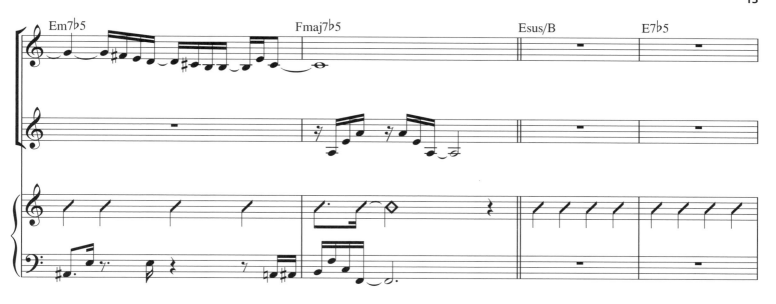

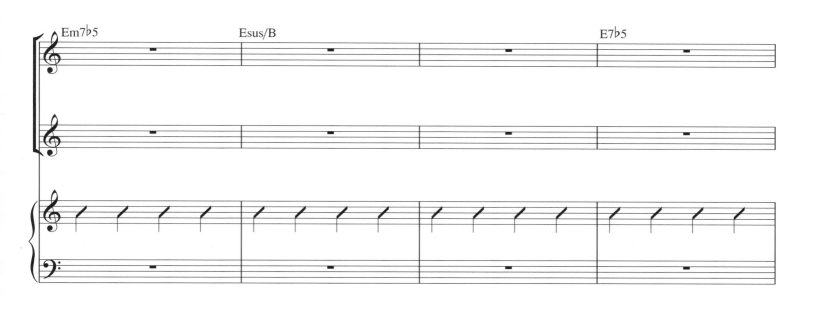

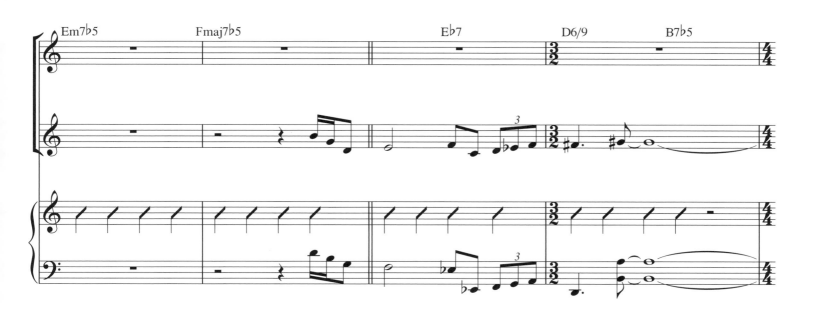

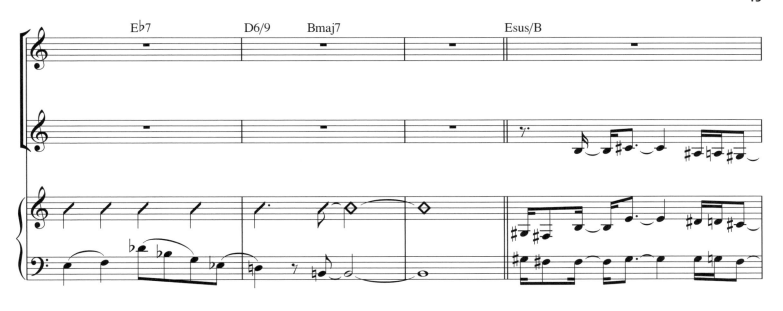

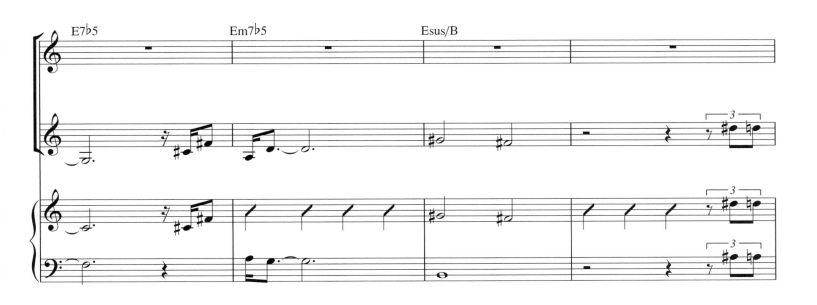

18

REALLY VERY SMALL

By ESPERANZA SPALDING

CHACARERA

By LEONARDO GENOVESE

Drum Solo

WILD IS THE WIND
from WILD IS THE WIND

Words by NED WASHINGTON
Music by DIMITRI TIOMKIN

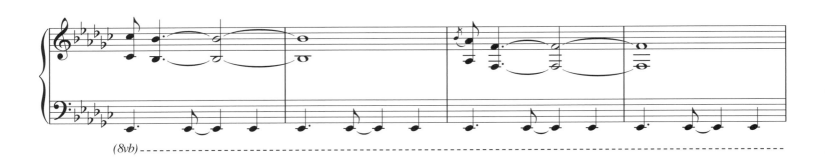

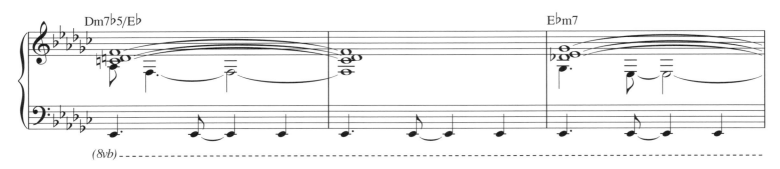

39

APPLE BLOSSOM

By ESPERANZA SPALDING

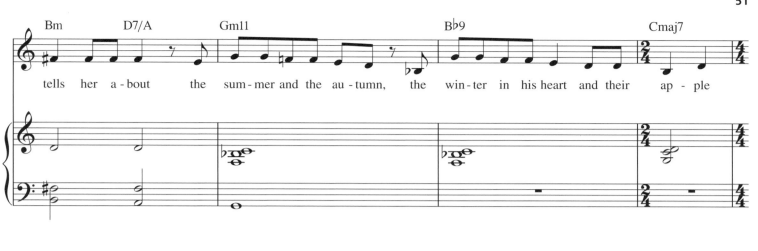

tells her a-bout the sum-mer and the au-tumn, the win-ter in his heart and their ap-ple

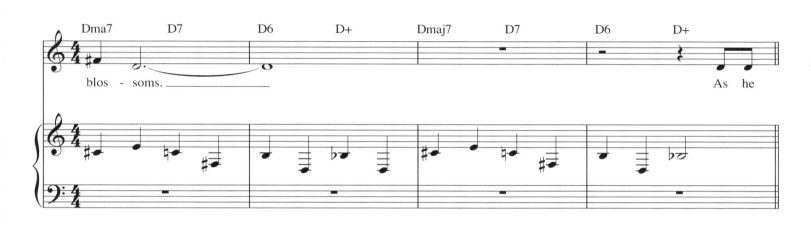

blos - soms. _____ As he

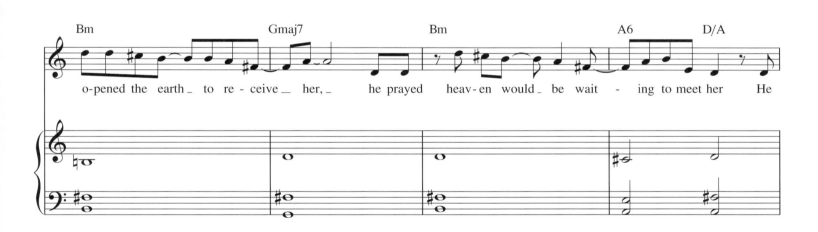

o-pened the earth _ to re-ceive _ her, _ he prayed heav-en would _ be wait - ing to meet her He

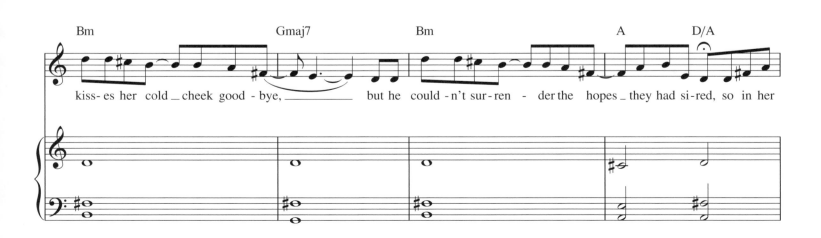

kiss-es her cold _ cheek good - bye, _____ but he could-n't sur-ren - der the hopes _ they had si-red, so in her

52

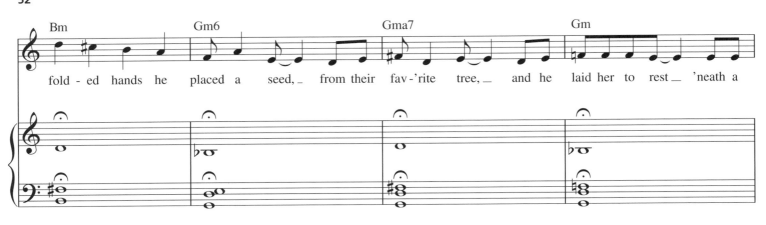

fold-ed hands he placed a seed,_ from their fav-'rite tree,_ and he laid her to rest_ 'neath a

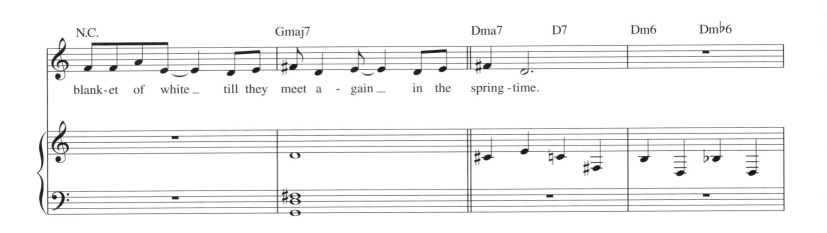

blank-et of white_ till they meet a - gain_ in the spring-time.

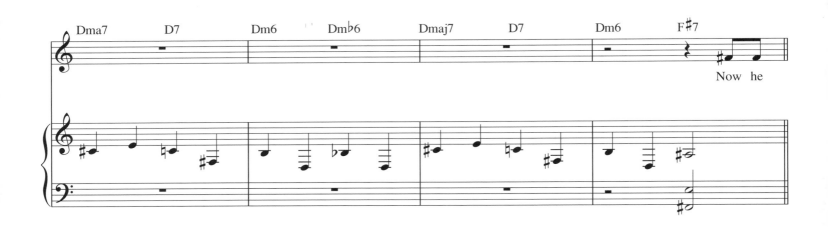

Now he

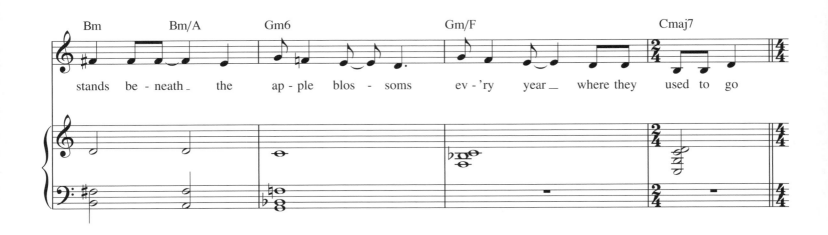

stands be - neath_ the ap - ple blos - soms ev - 'ry year_ where they used to go

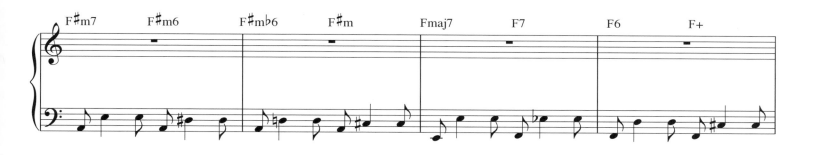

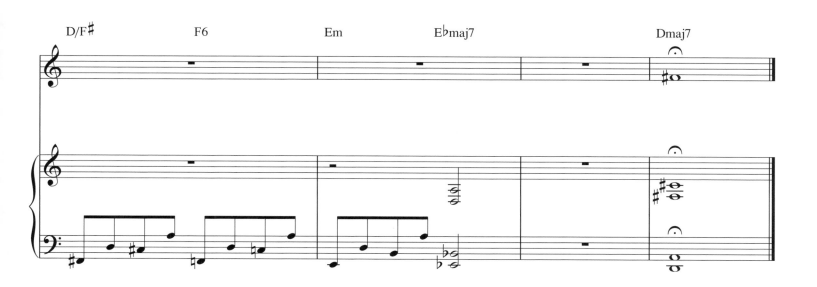

AS A SPROUT

By ESPERANZA SPALDING

WHAT A FRIEND

By ESPERANZA SPALDING

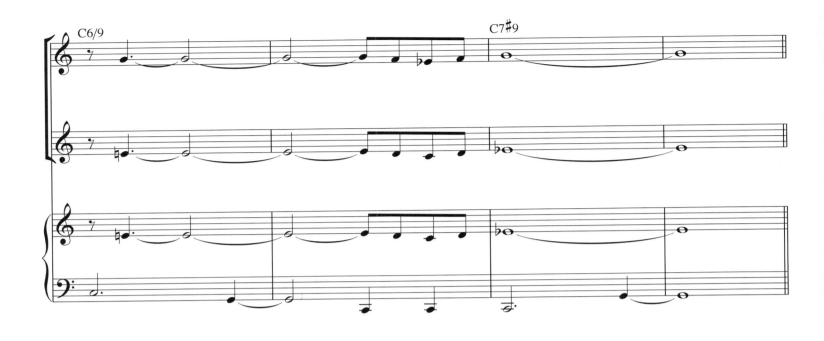

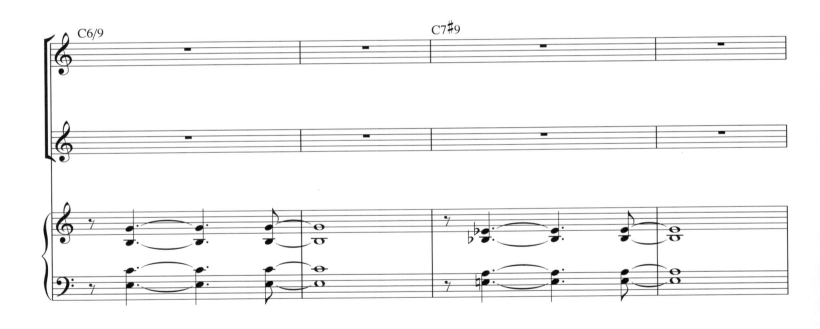

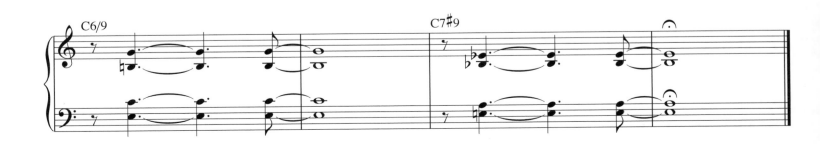

WINTER SUN

By ESPERANZA SPALDING

Up-tempo Samba

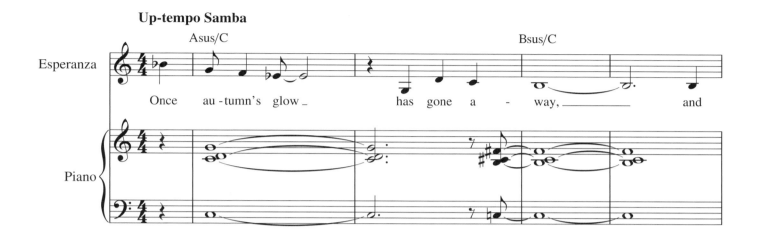

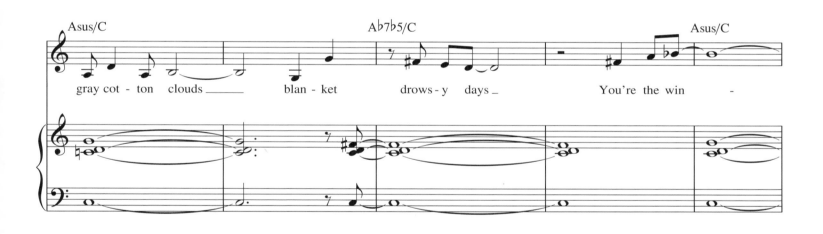

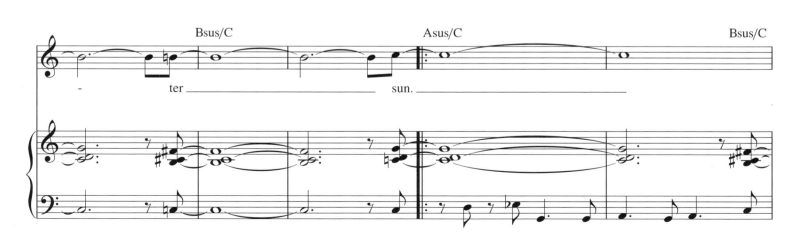

72

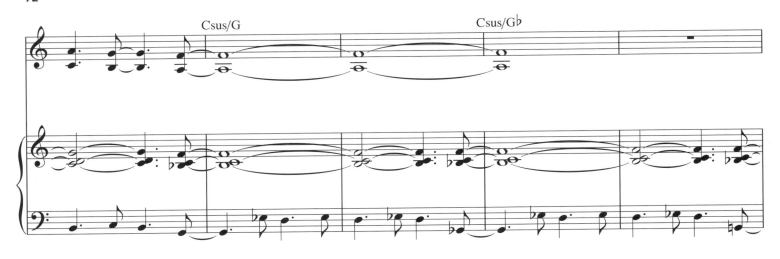

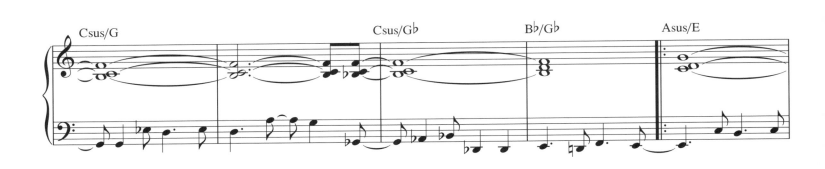

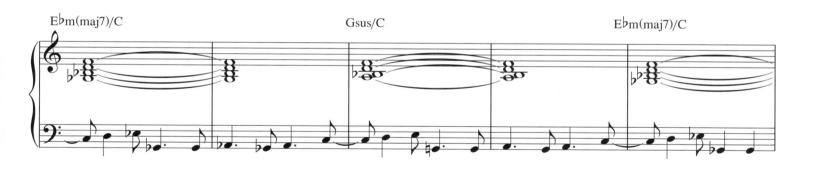

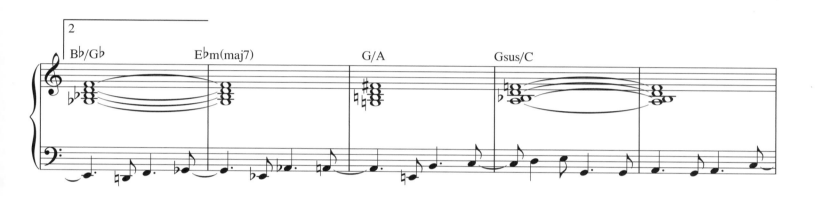

INÚTIL PAISAGEM

Music by ANTONIO CARLOS JOBIM
Portuguese Lyrics by ALOYSIO DE OLIVEIRA

Moderate Bossa nova

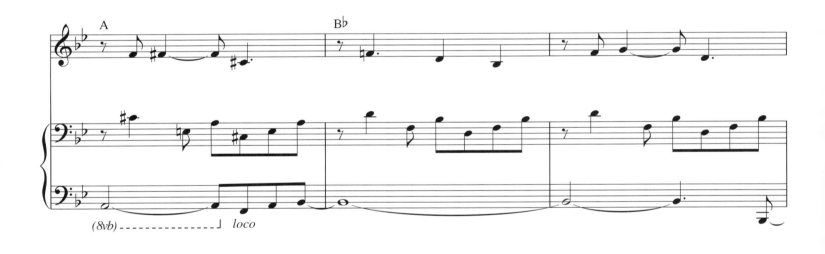

Syllables ad lib.

Mas ____ pra ____ que ____

pra que ____ tan - to céu ____ pra que tan -

82

SHORT AND SWEET

By ESPERANZA SPALDING

86

Gm♭6

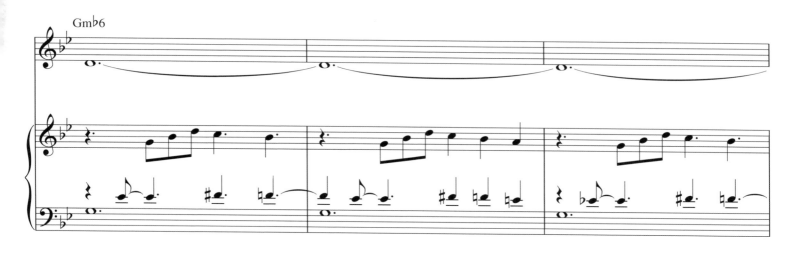